Never an Indian Bride

A Story of Shame, Guilt and Unspoken Dark Secrets

GYAN RUSSELL

First published by Ultimate World Publishing 2025
Copyright © 2025 Gyan Russell

ISBN

Paperback: 978-1-923255-81-4
Ebook: 978-1-923255-82-1

Gyan Russell has asserted her rights under the Copyright, Designs and Patents Act 1988 to be identified as the author of this work. The information in this book is based on the author's experiences and opinions. The publisher specifically disclaims responsibility for any adverse consequences which may result from use of the information contained herein. Permission to use information has been sought by the author. Any breaches will be rectified in further editions of the book.

All rights reserved. No part of this publication may be reproduced, stored in or introduced into a retrieval system, or transmitted in any form, or by any means (electronic, mechanical, photocopying, recording or otherwise) without the prior written permission of the author. Any person who does any unauthorised act in relation to this publication may be liable to criminal prosecution and civil claims for damages. Enquiries should be made through the publisher.

Cover design: Ultimate World Publishing
Layout and typesetting: Ultimate World Publishing
Editor: Vanessa McKay
Cover Image Copyright: SivaKumar N-Shutterstock.com

Ultimate World Publishing
Diamond Creek,
Victoria Australia 3089
www.writeabook.com.au

**I surrender myself to you Jesus.
You take care of everything.**

Dedication

This book is dedicated with love to my Nani, Amma and second mum for teaching me to be a better mum.

Testimonials

I have been blessed to know Gyan for 20 years and to call her a true friend. Through the many ups and downs of our lives, Gyan has been a constant source of inspiration and support.

Over the years, she has shared stories of her life—her pain, disappointments, and joys. With each conversation, the need to tell her story grew stronger. Gyan's courage in bringing her journey to life in this memoir is nothing short of inspiring.

The creation of Never an Indian Bride is a testament to her strength, resilience, and unwavering commitment to finding peace. Witnessing her journey has been both humbling and uplifting. Gyan's ability to embrace forgiveness over anger and to seek healing with grace and kindness is a rare and beautiful gift.

This book is a beacon of hope for anyone who has faced abuse or hardship. It stands as proof that with strength and courage, it is possible not only to heal but also to empower others through shared experience. Gyan, you are an amazing woman, and I am so proud of you. Thank you for allowing me to be part of your story.

With love, Deb Scott

TESTIMONIALS

Gyan's unwavering commitment to her personal growth and healing is nothing short of inspiring. Through remarkable courage and strength, she has prioritised aligning with her authentic self, embracing a heart-centred approach to life. This dedication has not only transformed her own journey but has also created a ripple effect of empowerment and healing for countless women in the Soul Space membership.

Her wisdom, authenticity, and active presence have uplifted and inspired so many of us. Now, through this heartfelt memoir, the transformative power of her story will extend even further—reaching and empowering people across the globe.

I am deeply in awe of the amazing, courageous, and wholehearted woman that Gyan is. Her journey reminds us all of the boundless possibilities that come from living with authenticity and intention.

Kelly Hine, Founder of Soul Space

Gyan's journey to writing Never an Indian Bride is nothing short of extraordinary. It's a testament to the transformative power of resilience and strength. After years of struggles, shame, and guilt, she has emerged with remarkable courage and conviction. This book is a beacon of hope, inspiring others to confront and share their truth with the world despite the fear of judgment.

Writing this book was an emotional roller-coaster as she relived her past and fought through buried pain. There were moments she wanted to give up, but her resilience—and perhaps something greater—helped her bring this powerful story to life.

Gyan's fun-loving, giving, and spiritual nature has been her strength throughout this journey. Her genuine honesty and hardworking spirit allowed her to confront her past with courage, while her deep spirituality helped her find the grace to let go and forgive. Through writing this book, she has not only shared her story but also grown into a stronger, freer version of herself, embracing her truth with humility and resilience.

I couldn't be prouder of her for sharing this story—not just for herself but for the many who will find hope and strength in her words. Personally, witnessing her growth this past year is proof of the transformative power of stepping into your authentic self.

Angela Jane, Founder of Travels of the World

TESTIMONIALS

Gyan's debut story is a profound testament to her resilience and extraordinary spirit. As her aunt and best friend, I have had the privilege of witnessing Gyan's transformation firsthand. Her writing is a masterful blend of raw honesty and poetic grace, capturing the essence of struggle and triumph with authenticity that is both heart-wrenching and inspiring.

Gyan's ability to articulate her inner battles and path to healing is nothing short of remarkable. Her words resonate deeply, offering solace and encouragement to anyone who has faced similar challenges. Through her story, Gyan not only shares her personal journey but also demonstrates that in our darkest moments, we often discover our greatest strength.

Her journey serves as a guide for those seeking to overcome their own obstacles. The courage it takes to share such a personal narrative is a true gift to the world, and I am incredibly proud of the woman she has become.

In closing, Gyan Russell is not just an author—she is an inspiration. Her story is a powerful testimony to the strength of vulnerability and the resilience of the human spirit. I wholeheartedly recommend her work to anyone in need of a reminder that they are never alone.

Rukhmani Nothelfer

This story is a testament to the incredible resilience of the human spirit. Gyan's journey inspires us to rise above our struggles and confront challenges with courage and determination. It is a deeply moving narrative that not only questions traditions but also challenges the way we perceive and connect with those we hold dear. Too often, we remain silent to preserve peace within our families, but there are moments when we must speak out, exhale the burdens we carry, and find the strength to let go.

Neelam Raj, High school educator

Gyan is an extraordinary individual whose friendliness, generosity, and capability shine through in everything she does. Her courage and adventurous spirit set her apart, and if she believes a seemingly impossible task can be achieved, you can proceed with full confidence. Her creative thinking and positive attitude consistently find a way to overcome challenges.

Gyan is deeply committed to her community, offering generous support to numerous activities and taking on difficult tasks with remarkable ease. She inspires and encourages those around her, fostering a sense of teamwork and determination.

Maureen Mosch

Contents

Dedication	v
Testimonials	vi
Introduction	1
Disclaimer	3
Chapter 1: Growing Up in Fiji	5
Chapter 2: Heartbreaking News	15
Chapter 3: Schooling	19
Chapter 4: Shame on the Family	27
Chapter 5: Marriage and Heartbreak	39
Chapter 6: Freedom	49
Chapter 7: Miracle - Higher Powers	55
Chapter 8: God Sent	67
Chapter 9: True Wedding Vows	71
Chapter 10: The Birth of a Motherhood	79
Chapter 11: Townsville & Travelling	107
Chapter 12: My Healing	179
Afterword	195
About the Author	197
Acknowledgments	201
Speaker Bio	205
Additional Information and Resources	207

Never an Indian Bride

Introduction

This is a story about resilience—the quiet yet unbreakable strength of the human spirit. It's a story of how we hold a remarkable power within us: the ability to heal, to rise from our traumas, and to reclaim our lives.

Trauma can leave deep scars, touching not only our emotions but also reshaping how we see ourselves, others, and the world around us. Sexual abuse can rob a person of their sense of safety, dignity, and trust. Yet healing is possible. Although it's a challenging journey, it's one that can be taken step by step, breath by breath.

Disclaimer

This book is about my personal experiences. In telling my story, I do not presume to tell the story of others who feature predominantly in this book.

Their feelings, emotions, thoughts and memories are their own and they deserve the respect I give them by only writing my story. This is my perspective only.

This book may trigger painful memories and or unusual reactions. Please see the back of this book for contact details and help available.

Chapter 1

Growing Up in Fiji

I was born on a small island in the South Pacific called Fiji to Indian parents who were also born there. My grandfather (Aja), had journeyed from India as an indentured labourer. In his youth, he married my grandmother (Aji) who had been married and had four children. Together, they had my father and my uncle.

My father often spoke of Aja's diligence and determination. Seizing the opportunity to buy inexpensive land, Aja purchased property for farming, initially cultivating sugarcane and later vegetables and rice. Remarkably, he even ventured back to India by ship with a friend, visiting his family before returning to Fiji. Aja was a devout, strict vegetarian Hindu. Although I never met him, the stories my family shared painted a vivid picture of a man I came to love and admire through their words.

I was born in Nausori Hospital, our local hospital, just a 15-minute drive away, in 1967. I am the fourth sibling, with three older sisters, a brother, and then a younger sister. When I was one-year-old, my mother experienced postnatal depression, and my aunt cared for me for six months during that time.

Surrounded by the warmth of my siblings, cousins, aunties, and uncles, I felt an abundance of love, especially from my grandmother, Nani. My school friends and teachers also contributed to a nurturing environment. Growing up on a farm, I was accompanied by many animals: dogs, cats, chickens, cows, horses, and pigs. Among them, my favourite was a cow.

I fondly recall my sisters teasing me about one of their teachers named Gyan, saying it sounded like my name. Their playful jests never bothered me, as they were always kind and loving. Our extended family visited frequently, and these gatherings were filled with joy and excitement. I especially loved the anticipation when Mum announced weekend visitors. Sometimes, we'd chase and catch a chicken to prepare for lunch or dinner. I was too scared to handle the chickens and couldn't bear to watch them being killed. My empathy for all living beings ran deep—a sentiment that endures to this day, especially in my longing for my pet cow.

Our farm sustained us, providing most of our food. We cultivated rice, which became a daily staple. I cherished the times spent with my family, planting rice seedlings in ankle-deep water. The mud and water made the work feel like play, and the shared effort brought us closer. Helping our parents on the farm, both indoors and out, was a part of life we embraced without complaint.

As we grew older and I started school, my sisters and I took on more responsibilities, often going to the farm alone to pick vegetables. Depending on the season, my father grew a variety of produce: eggplants, corn, lettuce, pumpkins, radishes, tomatoes, chilies, coriander, cucumbers, and more. Each harvest reflected the rhythm of the climate and the care we put into our land.

When I was about eight months old, an incident occurred that my sister and mother often recounted. We were visiting my aunt, my mother's sister, for a special celebration. My mother was sitting on the floor, frying puris (Indian bread) in a wok on a small kerosene stove. I was crying for her attention, so my elder sister placed me in my mother's lap. In the next moment, as my mother was taking the puris out, the wok, brimming with hot ghee, tipped over, spilling onto both of us. The pain and the ensuing screams were unimaginable.

I was rushed to Nausori Hospital. My father, who had stayed home, was devastated when he heard about the accident. I was left with a large, conspicuous scar on my right thigh. As I grew older, I was self-conscious about it, always keeping it covered and never wearing clothes that might reveal the scar.

When I was five years old, another mishap occurred. My mother asked me to go to the house next door to fetch something. I remember climbing the ten steps to the house, retrieving the item, and then falling from the top of the steps. After that, my memory went blank. I was taken to the hospital once more, and fortunately, I had no brain damage. My head was bandaged for a while, but that's all I recall. We had two houses: one for living in and the other for storing rice and other supplies.

I remember my primary school days fondly. We used to walk to school bare feet with siblings and friends. Every morning, my mum would wake up at 5 a.m. to cook breakfast for all of us. With unfailing dedication, she prepared our lunch: roti parcels filled with dry curry. My school days were filled with fun, playing with friends in the morning, at lunchtime, and sometimes after school, especially when we were training for netball games against other schools.

When I was in class two, my teacher tore my yellow folder that we had made to store our drawings. I was so upset; I thought she was being cruel to me, and I couldn't understand why. Later, I learned the real story. My dad was the treasurer of the school committee, and they had decided that my teacher had to go because she was no longer needed. Upset by this decision, she took her anger out on me just because my dad was involved. At the end of the year, when all the children received their folders, I didn't. I was devastated and couldn't understand why she did what she did until much later.

My dad was always involved at school. Once, he organised a concert where he was the main actor. He loved singing and performing, and he spoke three languages fluently, including English, Hindi and Fijian.

After finishing school, he dreamed of becoming a teacher, a noble ambition fuelled by his love for education. However, his mother had other plans. She insisted he help his father on the farm. He had worked tirelessly to complete his schooling, often walking miles in the mud, clad in gumboots, carrying an extra set of clothes, just in case. The road to education was difficult, but he loved school so much that he persevered.

Despite his aspirations, he inherited all the family land from Aja, as he was the only son left in Fiji. His brother had moved to England, leaving the responsibility of the farm solely to him. His two stepbrothers and two stepsisters received no land, even though Aja had helped raise and marry off all the children. The land was a symbol of wealth and status, and Aja was known for his riches.

The story of how my father met my mother is one of the fortunate ones. My uncle, my mother's eldest brother, worked in Suva, the capital of Fiji. My grandfather (Nana) insisted the only way my uncle could leave home to work in Suva was by finding a suitable husband for his eldest sister, who was 19 and ready to marry. Born in Navua in 1939, my mother was one of 11 children, with two sisters who had tragically died young. My Nani, who was married at the age of 12, was the only daughter.

My uncle began asking his colleagues if they knew any suitable boys for his sister. Someone mentioned my grandfather, noting that Aja was a wealthy man with extensive land holdings. A meeting was arranged, which was quite a journey in those days, although it now takes just over an hour by car.

My father was born in 1935, and my uncle a couple of years later, a man I had never met because he moved to the UK and had never returned to Fiji. He left Fiji before I was born. Growing up, I longed to meet this elusive uncle. To this day, we have had no success.

When my parents went out shopping or visiting relatives, my cousins, who lived next door, would come over to play. One hot day, while my parents were away, we decided to swim in the river, just a five-minute walk from our house. I was six years old and, at some point, began to drown. My cousin saved me, but the incident left me terrified of water. My parents often warned us not to swim in the river because a cousin had drowned there. This fear kept me out of the water for the next ten years, unable to put my head underwater.

My family was my world, the centre of everything. I always shared a double bed with one of my sisters. We never fought; we shared cleaning the house, doing dishes, and working outside. My favourite thing was gardening; I love flowers. We had a beautiful garden, and our grass was always green. We lived on the wet side of Fiji, which was much cooler than the western side.

At about eight, I started mowing the lawn with my dad. This was another job I enjoyed because I got satisfaction from seeing my hard work. We never watered the grass or the garden; enough rain fell from the sky. Sometimes, my sister and I used to steal cuttings from other people's front yards as we walked past because we were told that by stealing cuttings, plants grew well. I always picked flowers from my garden for the dining table.

My dad was given a lot of blocks of land by my Aja before he passed. As I was growing up, all the land was for farming, but slowly my dad sold block after block. Our house was built on 100-year lease land, so my Aja didn't own this land. People started building big, beautiful houses on the land they bought from my dad. I used to feel so envious of others having great big houses while we lived in an old house built by Aja.

After school, my sister and I used to go to the farm to pick vegetables. On the weekends, we would sell some by the side of the road and use the money to buy ice blocks, as it was always so hot. My resentment faded because those cold ice blocks made us happy. The shop where we bought them was owned by a family who bought the land from my dad.

My eldest sister had an Indian wedding at the age of 17. She finished form four at school and wanted to continue studying, but my dad said no; she had to get married. So, she did, to a man the family knew from our village who was living in Australia. My dad always said that there was no future in Fiji for young people. I was 10 years old when my favourite sister left for Melbourne with her husband. I loved her so much and was brokenhearted when she got married. We all missed her so much. I remember my mum telling us that my sister was going to have a baby. My nephew was born in December; he was a healthy, beautiful baby, and we were so excited to meet him.

We used to have so much fun with our cousins when my parents went away on the bus to visit friends or go shopping. We would quickly gather all our cousins from up the road and play ball games, laugh, and just be silly with each other. As soon as we saw the bus stop in front of our house, we would quickly pack everything away, and the cousins would run back home. I think my dad knew we were up to no good when he wasn't at home. Sometimes, my second sister would cook some sweets and hide them in the cupboard, and we would eat them later. My dad didn't like us playing ball games, listening to music, laughing, cutting our hair, or even painting our nails. He was so strict, and I used to fear him. I love my sisters and cousins so much.

Chapter 2

Heartbreaking News

My second sister got sick when she was 17. Her illness rendered her silent and immobile. I was only eleven and I remember our parents being deeply worried. Despite numerous medical consultations, the doctors found nothing physically wrong with her. Desperate for answers, our parents turned to spiritual solutions. They visited temples and consulted one witch doctor after another. One of the witch doctors claimed that someone had cast an evil spell on her out of jealousy because our older sister had married and moved overseas. The spell, meant for our older sister due to their shared first name, had unfortunately targeted her instead.

Every time my sister fell ill, she would sit still and silent. Our mother had to feed her by force, move her, and put her to bed. After a couple of weeks, she would start to recover, slowly beginning to eat, talk, and smile again. She always lost weight during her bouts of illness but would regain it once she started eating well again. Each time she returned to her normal self, we all felt immense relief and happiness. She would go back to school on the bus, as if nothing had happened.

One day, during one of her episodes, our cousin visited and mentioned knowing a powerful witch doctor who could cure her. Despite his assurances, my sister never fully recovered. Over the next two years, our cousin kept taking her to the witch doctor, but her condition remained unchanged. She would get sick for two weeks, recover for a while, and then fall ill again. My cousin repeatedly asked our father for money, claiming the witch doctor needed more funds to help her, and told my dad that all his children will die. Desperate for a solution, my father complied, but nothing improved. I grew increasingly angry at my sister for her illness and the suffering it caused our family. Our parents were in constant pain, and this became our new normal. We could predict the onset of her illness, and this cycle continued every two to three months for two years.

Life continued in its way. My sister stopped attending school and stayed home to help with housework.

HEARTBREAKING NEWS

One afternoon, while my parents, Kelly (third sister), my brother, and I were working on the farm not far from home, Bella, (youngest sister), who was seven, came running toward us. She shouted that my second sister was vomiting, and that we needed to come home immediately. We rushed back to find her unwell again. My father quickly called our uncle, who had a car, to take her to the hospital in Suva. The journey took about forty minutes, and my sister was admitted upon arrival. Everyone was distraught and at a loss for what to do next.

My sister had taken a bowl from the kitchen and went upstairs to the storage house next door. Bella followed her. My sister kept searching, her movements growing increasingly frantic until she found what she was looking for. She poured its contents into the bowl and drank it. Turning to Bella, she said she was sick of being sick and couldn't take it anymore. The bowl contained grass poison.

My sister was hospitalised for a few days but ultimately passed away, leaving us all heartbroken. When we received the news of her death, we were at our auntie's house. I remember standing frozen for a long time, paralysed by guilt and sadness. I had been angry with my sister for always being sick, not understanding the depth of her struggle.

My mum and dad were devastated but had to keep going, trying to live through the pain. We held a funeral for my sister. Our elder sister came with her husband and seeing her was a small comfort amidst the grief. I had missed her so much. For the next 25 years, I carried immense guilt, constantly asking myself why my sister did that to us. How did she even know the poison was in the house? I missed her deeply and dreamt about her all the time.

One day, at my lowest point mentally and physically, I finally understood why she did what she did. She was at her breaking point, and no one could help her get better. Once I realised this, I forgave both of us. She hadn't done it to hurt us; she was in unbearable pain. From that day on, I stopped dreaming about her. It felt like I had finally said goodbye to my beautiful sister.

Chapter 3

Schooling

I completed primary school in 1980, the same year my sister passed away. Despite the sorrow, my primary school years were a tapestry of joy, woven with the presence of amazing friends who felt like sisters. I cherished them all deeply. In Class 8, we faced the challenge of an entrance examination. Success in this exam allowed us to choose our high school based on our marks. My three closest friends and I excelled and were thrilled to apply to the schools we desired in Suva. Our excitement was boundless when we were all accepted into MGM High School. It felt like winning the lottery.

To celebrate our final day of primary school, our class organised a party filled with soft drinks, lollies, and cakes. We were filled with a mix of emotions, hugging each other tightly and promising to stay in touch forever.

At the end of the year, my dad had travelled to Melbourne to visit my eldest sister. With a hopeful heart, I asked my mum if I could attend school in Suva. To my delight, she agreed. The anticipation of joining my friends at our chosen school filled me with joy. When my dad returned, he brought back our three-year-old nephew. Our household buzzed with excitement; he was an absolute bundle of joy. Despite my nerves about my dad possibly insisting I attend the same high school my three older sisters had, he didn't. His approval made me feel special and incredibly happy.

The first day of high school was unforgettable. Dressed in a blue and white uniform lovingly sewn by my mother, I stepped into my first pair of school shoes and shouldered a brand-new bag brimming with books and stationery my father had thoughtfully bought. My mother had risen early to cook breakfast and prepare a roti parcel for my lunch. I caught the 7 a.m. school bus, joining three of my friends. The hour-long bus ride, followed by a ten-minute walk, was filled with laughter as we caught up after eight weeks of holidays.

As we arrived at the school, the air was electric. We eagerly explored our new classroom and met other students, feeling

SCHOOLING

the thrill of embarking on this new journey. The next chapter of our lives had begun, filled with new teachers, friends, subjects, expectations, standards, sports, and an abundance of boys to talk to and impress. At school, we were expected to always speak in the English language, while this was unacceptable at home.

Every day, I eagerly anticipated going to school, filled with a passion for learning new things. I felt incredibly fortunate to attend a prestigious Indian school in Suva, and I wore my pride in it like a badge of honour. Surrounded by the love of my friends, teachers, family, cousins, uncles, and aunties, I was excited about life and ready to embrace every opportunity to learn.

At home, my sister Kelly helped mum with domestic duties, while my brother and Bella walked to primary school by themselves. My dedicated dad spent his days on the farm.

During the December school holidays, while I was staying at my auntie's house, my dad received a letter from my new friend's brother addressed to me. When I returned home, my dad confronted me about it. I explained that My friend's brother must have got the address from his sister, as we had exchanged addresses to send Christmas cards to each other. Despite my explanation, he stopped me from returning to school. I was devastated, feeling lost and unsure of what to do next.

On the first day of school, my mum, Kelly and nephew were flying to Melbourne. We went to the airport to see them off, and as I watched them depart, I felt a deep sadness. Another sister was leaving me, and I knew I would miss Kelly's wedding in Melbourne. Upon returning from the airport, my dad surprised me with unexpected news: I could return to school the next day. I was overjoyed and immensely grateful.

The next morning, I woke up early, just like my mum, to prepare breakfast. I attempted to make roti for the first time. Despite its odd shape, I managed to get everyone fed and ready for school. Boarding the 7 a.m. bus, I felt a wave of happiness wash over me—school, friends, fun, laughter, and freedom. It was the best time of my life.

At home, I took on the responsibilities of cooking, cleaning, washing clothes by hand, while also keeping up with my studies. Though I was often exhausted, I felt a sense of accomplishment seeing the clean laundry hanging on the line. My beloved Nani would visit during the day, helping with the chores. She took two buses to come and stay with us, always there to support us. I loved my Nani deeply; she had a beautiful soul, always helping her children and grandchildren.

One important lesson I learned from my Nani at a young age was her dedication to her family. No matter how unhappy her children were with each other, she visited them all, giving each her precious time. She never stayed still, always travelling and helping others. I still miss her so much.

Nani would stay with us for a week or two at a time, bringing a welcome respite from the daily chores. But after she left, the weight of all the chores fell squarely on my shoulders. One fateful day, I fell terribly ill. I remember lying on my mum's bed, the throbbing pain in my head making everything feel unbearable. *I can't do this anymore*, I thought, feeling overwhelmed and desperate. *Please, Mum, come back quickly.* I suffered a headache for an entire week, and though every fiber of my being wanted to stay in bed, I somehow dragged myself up and returned to the routine of schooling.

When my mum finally returned after three long months, I was overjoyed. Her arrival meant I could now focus on my studies. It was then, at 15 years old, that I truly realised how much I appreciated my mum for taking care of all of us. I spoke to her about everything and anything. Mum and I shared a special bond; we cherished each other's company.

I was thoroughly enjoying my school life, even though it took me a bit longer than my friends to understand some concepts. What mattered to me was my love of learning. Sometimes, I finished my schoolwork on the bus because I didn't understand the questions. My friends were always there to help, especially with balancing the accounting ledger. I often daydreamed, wishing my sisters were there to help me.

My mum's story was different. She had to leave school when she was in class three to take care of her siblings and never had the opportunity to really learn how to read or write. Sometimes, she would come and sit at the table, and I would help her practice writing her name and numbers from one to ten. The smile on her face was unmistakable; she loved learning.

Mum was a tireless worker, her hands constantly busy sewing clothing for others and tending to our flock of chickens whose eggs and meat she sold to earn a steady income. Her diligence ensured that her wallet was never empty. Dependable and generous to a fault, Mum never hesitated to say yes to any request I made. When my school fees were overdue and Dad hadn't paid them, it was Mum I turned to for help. She always provided the money, trusting me to repay her once Dad came through.

At the end of the school year party, I asked Mum if she could make puris, the delightful Indian bread, for the entire class. Ever the devoted parent, she rose at 5:00 a.m., her hands moving deftly through the familiar motions of mixing, rolling, and frying. By 7:00 a.m., a mountain of golden, puffy puris was packed and ready for me to take to school.

Mum was like Nani in that way—always ready to lend a hand wherever she went. At prayer gatherings, Indian weddings, parties, and other celebrations, she would be there, cooking alongside the other aunties and friends, filling the air with the rich aromas of our heritage. She was an amazing cook, her dishes infused with the love and care that defined her. This was the time when I'd watch the beautiful brides dressed in their colourful saris, and I'd dream of becoming a bride one day. As I grew older, I realised I had inherited this natural talent from Nani and mum. Watching them, learning from their expertise, I discovered my passion for cooking. Eventually, this love for our culinary traditions led me to open my curry business, a tribute to the generations of skilled, nurturing women who had come before me.

Dad, on the other hand, wasn't very approachable. Twice I turned to my dad for help with my homework, but he would always respond with, "you should know that," so I eventually stopped asking him. I was terrified of my dad's reaction if he found out the trouble I was in at school once. So, I lied to the teacher who wanted to meet him. It all started because one of my best friends from primary school accused me of finding a boyfriend for her. She had gone out during lunchtime to the shop, returned late, and dragged me into her mess. When the teacher asked why she was late, she blamed me.

That Monday morning, the teacher called me into the office to tell me what my friend had said. He demanded that I bring my dad to the office. My friend had her mum with her, and I was shocked by the whole story. I went back to class, thinking, "No way am I bringing my dad here." He would stop me from going to school, so I decided not to tell him.

For a week, the teacher kept hustling me every morning. I kept saying my dad was too busy on the farm. Finally, he gave me a warning: he wanted to see my dad on Monday, or I had to go back and get him.

Monday morning came, and when he called me into the office, I said again that my dad was busy on the farm. He told me to go back and get him. As I walked back to the classroom, crying, my biology teacher stopped me and asked why I was crying. I told her about my dilemma.

The biology teacher went to the office and explained my story to the Assistant Principal. They let me go back to class with no need to bring my dad. A beautiful soul had saved my life.

My friend stopped coming to school for three months because she was unwell. Meanwhile, I studied hard and passed my form four exam with good marks. I was so excited because none of my sisters before me had passed this exam. I was incredibly proud of myself for this achievement and my family was pleasantly surprised as well.

Chapter 4

Shame on the Family

Approaching my third year of high school with a sense of pride, I could feel the excitement my future held. I was going to be the first to finish school and go to college. I was determined to make something of my life. With high hopes and a dream of teaching children, it was so close I could almost touch it. In my dreams, I saw myself teaching, falling in love with an Indian boy, marrying him, having children, and settling down in Fiji. I never in my wildest dreams saw myself leaving the country of my birth and going overseas like my sisters.

I was thriving in school, my excitement bubbling over each day. I had many friends. We were cheeky, full of life, and always acting silly, especially when our school bus stopped at different schools to drop off and pick up other kids. I vividly remember one day when a boy threw a letter to me as the bus paused to let more students on - he confessed he liked me. My friends and I couldn't stop laughing; I did not know he had been watching me. Those were the fun days.

Then the unthinkable happened, changing my life forever.

One day, while at home with my brother, my parents and Bella took a trip to town by bus. A family friend often visited our house before going to help on the farm, usually on school days. However, he arrived to pick up my brother this Saturday. They left together, while I was engrossed in my studies at the dining table in the lounge with the back door locked.

Hours passed, and I was having a wonderfully productive day when the friend returned for a glass of water while my 13-year-old brother was still at the farm. I hadn't noticed his approach until he was at the front door, so I hurried to the back of the house to fetch the water.

As I was returning, I saw him walking towards me with a determined look on his face. The next minute he grabbed my wrist with such force I was frozen. When he threw me onto my mum's bed, it was like my mind couldn't keep up with real time. I couldn't believe what was happening.

This man we have known for so long is going to hurt me. I knew nothing about male and females being intimate. When I was 16, nothing was ever spoken about what happened between a man and a woman. He was a strong man, and I couldn't fight back. He raped me and left immediately. I saw blood in my underwear, as I still had it on and panicked. So many thoughts raced through my mind; I was scared and confused. What just happened? And all I can remember was my elders telling me to be careful out there. Is this what we should be scared of and why we should not talk to boys for fear of someone forcing themselves on us?

In shock, I awkwardly stood in my mum's room in the quiet of the afternoon, thinking about what had just happened to my body. My mind was a storm of confusion, fear, and anger. I felt a deep ache, a sadness that settled in my bones, making me feel dirty and scared. My voice froze.

Every time this monster entered my house for the next three months to work on the farm, I stood frozen in sheer panic and fear. I would stare at him, hoping my pain, internal wounds and fear were evident in my eyes. He had no comprehension of the havoc he had unleashed on my peace of mind. It was extremely difficult to function, let alone speak or even move.

At that moment, no words were sufficient or even close to being able to express the never-ending terrifying emotions swirling through my mind. All I knew was that my safe space had been violated.

I kept the events of the past months a BIG secret hidden deep within! Keeping this secret locked inside me seemed of the utmost importance. I kept thinking it must be my fault somehow. Did I smile too nicely or was I too friendly towards him? I wanted to stay at home and study. Why didn't I just go to town with my parents? I should have left the back door open so at least I could have run outside and saved myself. These words kept repeating in my mind. These words haunted me for years.

As weeks passed by, I felt sick! Daily morning nausea, that would go away by lunch, occurred out of the blue. My stomach grew bigger. What was happening to me? Is there a baby growing in my belly? I only came to this idea, as I knew a big stomach on a lady meant a baby inside. I had seen pregnant women before walking around with big stomachs.

I continued going to school, carrying this burden, feeling alone and lost. And now, as my body changed, fear took hold. I prayed to my Gods, pleading for help. Please Gods, I don't want this baby. Take it away from me.

I felt guilt like a heavy rock in my chest, as if I had done something wrong and this was my punishment. Months passed before my mother noticed. She saw the signs, the missed periods, and my growing belly. Worried, she called for the village midwife, a woman known for her wisdom. The midwife confirmed what my mother feared. I was pregnant.

My mother, with a mixture of anger and fear, asked me the question that shattered the silence: who did this to you? I told her the name of the monster, a man known to both of us. My mother then asked if I wanted to marry him!!!!!

My voice was frozen, unable to explain, unable to understand how to voice the horror of what had happened.

The monster who had hurt me was already married, with a child of his own. The question haunted me for years: you are asking me if I want to marry him? I couldn't comprehend it. The injustice of being asked to bind myself to the man who had taken so much from me.

In that quiet moment, the weight of what had happened settled on my shoulders. I felt a pain that words could not describe, a pain that I carried silently, hidden from the world.

I hadn't invited him in. I didn't ask for his presence, but there he was, standing in my living room. His intrusion was like a harsh reminder of the frailty of safety and control. There must have been a mistake, a misunderstanding, for him to be here. But how does one speak in such a situation? Words failed me, trapped in my throat.

The silence between my mum and I was thick and heavy with unspoken words. I tried to express the violation I felt, the fear, but my mind was blank, my voice lost in the chaos of emotions. How could I explain this to someone who hadn't experienced it? How could I make them understand the vulnerability of a shattered sanctuary?

It felt like every door around me was slammed shut, trapping me in a cage of despair. The weight of the shame I had brought upon my family was so overwhelming that I wished the earth would swallow me whole. The thought of ending my life became a tempting escape, though I couldn't figure out how to do it.

I was drowning in a sea of sadness, abandoned by those I needed most. I started questioning God, wondering why He allowed men who inflict so much unbearable pain on others, to exist. My mind and heart were broken, and with no support from anywhere, I was lost in my dark thoughts. But I had to survive. Somehow, I stopped blaming God and started asking for help.

The most vivid memory I have is of my mother, her voice full of anger and disappointment. Our relationship, once a source of comfort, had fractured irreparably. She was so disappointed. She, too, had shared my dream of finishing school, getting a job, and building a better life for myself. But she stopped speaking to me, stopped asking questions, and stopped caring about my side of the story. The silence between us was louder than any argument. All I wanted was to end my suffering and reunite with my late sister. My mother's constant anger was a storm I couldn't withstand, and it seemed there was no escape. All I wanted was for her to hold me and take my pain away.

I continued attending school, holding my secret tightly inside. I didn't speak to any of my friends or teachers. Looking back, I realised I had only one source of support: God. He was there showing me his light and I prayed to him morning, day, and night. Each time I glanced at my growing belly, I whispered a desperate plea: "Please, God, make my stomach stop growing."

As soon as I completed my final exam in Form Five, I stopped attending school in November. There was no chance to say farewell to my friends or teachers, no celebration to mark the end of the school year. I felt an overwhelming sense of failure, as though I had let everyone down: myself, my parents, my siblings, my cousins, my uncles and aunts, my friends, and my teachers. I felt the weight of my cousins' laughter, each giggle a dagger of isolation. No one knew what to say, and I felt utterly alone.

Leaving my beloved home was a heart-wrenching ordeal, but I had no choice. I was taken to my uncle's house in Suva, where my days would be filled with caring for the children and working in the shop, keeping myself both occupied and safe.

In December, my mother took me to a private doctor in Suva, concealed from prying eyes, where I gave birth. The details of those hours are lost to me, a blur of pain and confusion. The only thing that stands out is the cry of a baby in my uncle's house as I was taken to my room. My body felt numb, my heart frozen. I never saw or held the baby, not that I wanted this baby. How was I ever going to love this baby? When I opened my eyes after a while, there was no crying of the baby. The baby died. I didn't know what the intention of my family was about the baby, but there was talk to abort or adopt out. I was told later my auntie and uncle were going to adopt the baby. But unfortunately, or fortunately, the circumstances did not allow it! Maybe that's what God wanted?

For days, I laid in bed, convinced I was dying. I could not speak, and food no longer interested me. One day, I heard someone in the house say I was so ill that I might die. I wanted to rise, to prove them wrong, but my body didn't allow me. I was too weak to move.

It was at that moment of weakness that I accepted my fate. I was ready to die, and the fear that I had felt disappeared.

I can't recall how my recovery began, as if my memory had been wiped clean. One day, I found myself well again, eating normally and doing my everyday chores. My father visited occasionally, always bringing cod liver oil tablets, thinking they would make me strong again. In his way, this was an expression of love. I believe God gave me strength and my dad's love helped me heal. I don't remember my mother visiting. She seemed too consumed by disappointment and anger, preoccupied with managing the household.

Nani was a beacon of warmth and love in this sea of disappointment. I don't know if she realised how much she helped me, but her kindness was a soothing balm to my broken, aching heart.

Six months later, Nani passed away from stomach cancer. In that short time, I felt the weight of everything I had missed—moments, conversations, and the simple comfort of her presence. Losing her was the deepest sorrow, as her kindness was a lifeline in my deepest despair, that her acceptance and love had only just started to heal a tiny, tiny piece of the broken shards that were once my joyful heart. This was a reminder of the fleeting nature of time and the importance of cherishing those we love.

I am immensely grateful for my uncle and aunt, who welcomed me into their home. Despite having four young children and running a grocery shop, they found room for me. Helping at the shop kept me busy and away from harmful thoughts. Looking back, I'm thankful my parents sent me here, as it meant I was still alive and living.

My aunt, who had cared for me when I was a baby, also lived at my uncle's house. Every day was a storm of activity, starting at 5 a.m. and ending only after 11 p.m. This chapter of my life was a good one. I buried my pain in the business of my work and did what needed to be done. I accepted my circumstances and found that I had the energy to meet each day's demands.

My favourite memory from this time was walking my little cousin to her kindergarten. On the way back, I savoured a sense of freedom that made my heart leap. It was a moment of pure joy that I cherish deeply.

As I grew up, I was constantly warned about the dangers of walking to school alone. "Watch out for strangers," they would say, especially those drinking alcohol by the roadside or lurking in the bushes. But as the years went by, I discovered a deeper, more unsettling truth: feeling safe within the confines of my own extended family was a challenge.

One of my cousins would come to my home and would look at me which made me feel uncomfortable, and I made sure that I was not alone. He was touching my private parts for months when I was 15. It usually happened when he found me alone at his house. Despite being constantly conscious of my safety, I was sometimes caught off guard. He would follow me into the bedroom when my aunt asked me to fetch something. I know now that was sexual abuse, which I didn't know when I was 15. After the rape happened, he never came near me, as I was living in a house full of people.

I remained silent, weighed down by the societal belief that females are always at fault.

In the shadows of silence, I found a sense of safety, carefully avoiding danger. But in my solitude, I felt the weight of the unspoken words, a loud silence where courage should have risen and fought for justice.

In the depths of my soul, I harboured the secrets of betrayal, where trust was twisted into pain. I was an innocent child who had experienced darkness and pain without a thought for the victim, the youth that had been stolen from me along with all my dreams, hopes and wishes.

It felt as though the criminal, these monsters, could just take and take whatever they wished and keep living in our society with no justice done, whilst my suffering seemed insurmountable.

As I walked the unforgiving streets, I silently prayed, thankful for the protection that spared me from physical harm. But fate had a cruel twist, as those closest to me inflicted wounds that cut much deeper than any physical pain.

A couple of years ago, I was out at an event, feeling happy when the phone rang. It was my dad, and his voice was serious. "He's gone," he said. I was confused.

"Who?" I asked, my heart racing.

"The one who inflicted pain upon our family," he replied. I had to ask for his name. Who was this person? His words were so heavy I couldn't comprehend.

At that moment, a storm of emotions hit me. But as the truth dawned on me, I realised the gravity of his words. It wasn't just the family who had suffered; it was me—my life had been scattered to the wind and altered forever. His actions had nearly destroyed me, praying for my life to end so many times I lost count. Was my family even truly aware of how much pain and suffering I had gone through because of his action? After I finished talking to my dad, I didn't know how to feel. All I ever wanted was love and support, and the understanding that it wasn't my fault. Whether he was alive, or dead, didn't change my pain.

Chapter 5

Marriage and Heartbreak

At 17 and a half, my parents informed me I would be going to Australia to get married. I didn't argue; I merely complied with their decision. My mother picked me up from my uncle's house, and we went shopping. With the modest savings I had earned from working in a shop, I bought my first pair of gold earrings—something I had longed for since childhood. Gold, my mum often said, symbolised wealth. She used to tell me that whoever would care for me in my old age would inherit her gold. I also purchased a small brown suitcase and some clothing. After eight months away, I returned home. I felt lost, empty, frightened, and unsure of what to do or say.

On the day of my departure, I was at the airport with a half-empty brown suitcase, containing only a few belongings. My cousin and parents had driven me to Nadi for my first international trip, a journey that seemed to stretch on endlessly. Throughout the drive, a numbness enveloped me. I had no desire to go to Australia or to marry a stranger; all I wanted was for my mum and dad to hold me, to keep me safe. This was my first flight on a large airplane, and I was petrified. I sat frozen in my seat, the untouched dinner before me, and spoke to no one.

I arrived in Melbourne on the freezing night of July 31st. My sister picked me up from the airport, and I was overjoyed to see her. Being reunited with my favourite sister made me feel a bit safer. However, I disliked Melbourne from the start. On my first night, the bed felt wet, a shock in the middle of winter. I missed my family, my country, the warm weather, and my language. I felt sad and lonely, struggling with my limited English and always fearing I would say something wrong. To improve my English, I was advised to watch television, which helped significantly.

Soon after, I was introduced to my future husband. We were to marry in a few months. I was instructed not to share my story with him, and so I didn't. I felt ashamed and guilty, burdened by the secret. I did not want to marry this man, but I felt I had no choice.

MARRIAGE AND HEARTBREAK

Before I got married, another nightmare began. I realised I wasn't safe here either. I didn't know what to do or where to go. My voice was frozen once again. The man of the house started grooming me. I was scared and vulnerable, placing all my trust in the household, believing I would be cared for. That trust was horribly misplaced. I was in danger again. He took me shopping, hoping no one would see us together. Then at home when no was at home, he would make me lay down in bed next to him. He raped me whenever we were alone in the house. I trusted him to be on my side, but he told me not to tell anyone, claiming he did it because it had already happened to me before. I felt sick to my stomach. He told me not to tell my sister. I knew this was so wrong.

I was so scared. To be truthful, I didn't want to be sent back to Fiji, even though I missed my family and my country. Something inside me urged me not to return. At that time in my life, I was merely surviving. I never thought of committing suicide; I just kept going. My thoughts were filled with questions: Why was this happening to me again? What had I done wrong to deserve this?

After being rejected by my family in Fiji, I came to Melbourne, hoping to feel safe, but that security eluded me once more. I felt so guilty that I couldn't confide in my sister, as the predator had warned me to stay silent. I buried the dark secret deep within and continued living. I was constantly on guard, always looking to protect myself from the predator. Every minute of the day, I made sure someone else was in the house with me.

My wedding was arranged in just six weeks. When I met my future husband for the first time, I felt nothing toward him. I was numb, filled with feelings of deceit, shame, guilt, and sadness. I went along with everything I was told. It was a white wedding held at a hotel with a small number of guests. I can't say that I disliked my husband; he was kind to me. His family's love was a blessing, and I thought that at least I would feel safe with him. My upbringing taught me that once you get married, you stay with your husband no matter what happens.

My husband was every bit the gentleman, always treating me with kindness and respect. Yet, despite his considerate nature, I felt no love for him, nor did I feel any affection for myself. Internally, I was tormented. I saw myself as damaged goods, handed over to someone pure and unsuspecting. Emotionally drained, I had nothing to offer him. I merely went through the motions, fulfilling the role expected of me as a wife. Resignation set in as I convinced myself that safety, food, and shelter were enough. What more could I possibly need?

During the days I spent at home, without the obligations of work, a predator would often appear at my doorstep, seeking opportunities. Whenever I glimpsed his car approaching, I would immediately retreat, concealing myself within the house and pretending to be absent. My front window curtains were always drawn, a deliberate precaution. I didn't own a car so there was no clear indication of my presence. He would knock persistently, scrutinising the house, but eventually, he would leave. Each time, I silently thanked God that he never realised I was inside.

After two months of being homebound, I finally secured a job at the Biro Bic factory. The mix of excitement and nerves was noticeable as I prepared for my first day. My commute involved catching two buses, a journey that was both daunting and exhilarating. With a keen eye on the timetable, I made sure to arrive punctually, feeling a surge of pride in my newfound independence.

The factory job involved packing pens, razor blades, and lighters into packets on a conveyor belt, a task that required speed and precision. I quickly learned the importance of ensuring no plastic bags went empty, a measure to minimise waste. Alongside me on the conveyor belt were three other women, all of whom welcomed me warmly. They were curious about my background, asking questions I could only respond to with a few words because of my limited English. This language barrier turned out to be a blessing, sparing me from divulging my darkest secrets.

One day, the boss assigned me to another section to help with packing lighters. It was there that I met a lady from

India, Helen. This was her first job in the country too, and we struck up a conversation that revealed many shared experiences. She had fled her home and entered into a marriage due to her strict father. Our shared histories of escape and self-imposed penance created an immediate bond between us. We found peace in each other's stories, realising that we were not alone in our struggles and regrets.

My marriage only lasted eighteen months. I was devastated, crying myself to sleep every night, feeling the sting of rejection once again. Fear consumed me as I faced an uncertain future. My greatest terror, however, was the predator who haunted my thoughts, leaving me desperate to find a way to keep myself safe. I bore this dark secret alone, hiding it from my sister—the one person I had believed could protect me.

By this time, I had switched to a new job that was just a ten-minute walk from the unit I had lived in when I was married. However, circumstances forced me to move back to my sister's house. This was a difficult period when the predator would drop me off at work each day. Every morning, I felt sick to my stomach, praying fervently for God to just get me to work safely, and every morning, my prayers were answered.

Since I didn't drive at the time, I devised a plan to ensure my safety. My sister's friend, Charlie, lived within walking distance of my new job, and I asked if I could stay with her. God must have been listening to my prayers because my sister agreed. It was the best day of my life so far.

Charlie welcomed me warmly and gave me a room. I paid for a board and helped with dinner and chores around the house. Charlie had two beautiful boys who kept me busy and brought joy to my days. She was like an earth angel to me, and for the first time in a long while, I began to feel happy again.

Work had become a place of camaraderie and joy. I started making friends with both men and women, and everyone was incredibly kind to me. Lunchtime became a cherished part of the day, where we would sit together, talk, tell jokes, tease each other, laugh, and sometimes act downright silly. It was amazing how much fun work could be with such a wonderful company.

Around this time, my friend Helen mentioned a job opening at her workplace. I applied and got the position at a place called Stegbar. As my last day at my current job approached, I was filled with mixed emotions. My coworkers gave me a beautiful present, which made me feel both happy and sad to be leaving them. There was also a bouquet of flowers on the table with a card that read, "From your secret admirer." My heart leapt, and I immediately thought it must be from Robert, the guy who had been talking to me for a while. When I thanked him later, he assured me it was not from him.

Curious, I asked around and discovered it was from a young guy who often sat with us at lunch. I thanked him, feeling humbled and touched by the fact that people liked me and enjoyed being around me. This young man expressed his interest in going out with me, but I knew I couldn't commit to him.

Leaving my old job was bittersweet, but I carried with me the warmth of the friendships I had made and the memories of the laughter and joy that had filled my days.

I found myself back at my sister's house, consumed with anger and frustration. My life had been on an upward trajectory, and now it felt like I was back at square one. The incident that triggered this setback was so trivial. A guy who often joined us at lunchtime was taking a walk, and when he saw me in the front yard of Charlie's house, he stopped to say hello. I introduced him to Charlie, we had a brief chat, and then he continued on his way.

A couple of weeks later, I was abruptly told to move back to my sister's house. When I asked why, the answer stunned me: it was because a man had visited me. Had I known the consequences, I would have pretended not to know him. I was devastated. The day I had to leave, Predator came to pick me up. I was alone at Charlie's house, expecting my sister, and utterly unprepared for what was about to happen.

Once more, he orchestrated his vile intentions and violated my body again. I was 20 years old, overwhelmed with self-disgust, and powerless to protect myself.

I vowed to myself that this would never happen again. I didn't tell my sister; fear kept me silent. I harboured the dark secret, pretending nothing had transpired.

I poured all my energy into learning how to get my licence. In the meantime, as I put it, the Predator had to drive me to work every day. My morning prayers became a litany: "Please, God, keep me safe. Please, God, let us get straight to work." I remember repeating this ritual daily until I finally earned my licence and got my own car. The pride I felt in that small achievement was immense. With my own vehicle, I felt a newfound sense of safety on my morning drives to work. The sense of empowerment grew within me. This boost in confidence inspired me to save for furniture, with dreams of moving into my own place, then I knew I would be alright.

At work, I began forming beautiful friendships. I yearned to share my inner suffering, but the fear of judgement kept me silent. Instead, I carried my dark secret, burdened by guilt. During this time, my friend Helen often reminded me that Jesus forgives us all, no matter what we've done in the past. Her words about Jesus were a constant in my life.

Despite my internal struggles, I couldn't let any man come close to me, no matter how kind they were. Young men at work frequently invited me out, but I always declined, though I was only twenty and enjoyed the company of funny, cheeky, and interesting men. Then, out of nowhere, I received a beautiful bouquet at work. The card bore a phone number and a simple message: he wanted to see me. It was from Robert.

Curious, I called him and asked him to meet me during my lunch break one day. Sitting in his car, I remember feeling so cold that we just chatted for twenty minutes before I had to return to work. He gave me a gentle kiss on the cheek and left. Robert would call me at home, and we would chat about work and life. After a few calls, I was told by the predator to stop speaking with him. Angry and feeling powerless, I called him and bluntly told him not to contact me again because my family forbade it. Immediately after, I felt terrible, imagining how heartbroken he must have been. Years later, I tried to find him to apologise, but my search was unsuccessful.

I was back in the trap - my destiny controlled by him.

Chapter 6

Freedom

One day, in 1987, we received a phone call from my uncle with distressing news: my sister Kelly was in trouble. He explained that she wanted to leave her husband and return to the family. She had been trapped in an abusive marriage and had three children. For four long years, she had no contact with any of us, leaving us in the dark about her life and her wellbeing. We were all deeply worried about her safety. Upon hearing the news, I felt an overwhelming sense of relief and joy, as I had missed her terribly. I hadn't seen her since she left Fiji five years ago.

One night, my uncle and aunt drove for two hours to her place in country Victoria to help her pack some clothes and baby supplies. They then drove two hours back to my sister's house, providing a safe haven away from her husband. My heart soared with happiness at the sight of her and the kids, but I was equally devastated by the fear etched on her face. I just wanted to take her pain away. She didn't need to say a word; I understood her suffering. All she needed at that moment was to stay safe and keep the children safe. We all knew the challenges that lay ahead, and fear rose among us as we felt like we had kidnapped her.

I buried my pain deep inside to support Kelly and her children. The presence of family members in the house brought a sense of security. A few days later, when her husband returned from Melbourne, he came to my sister's house looking for his wife and kids. He intended to take them back home. Kelly, showing immense bravery, told him it was over. I was terrified he would force his way into the house and take them away. I remember screaming at him and his pregnant girlfriend. Kelly never went back to him. Now, four adults and four children were living in a three-bedroom house, navigating the complexities of this new chapter in our lives.

This turn of events marked the beginning of my plans to move out of my sister's house. Kelly and I started diligently saving so we could find a place of our own. Meanwhile, my mother arrived from Fiji to stay with us for a few months, which brought the total number of people in the house to nine.

FREEDOM

Seizing the moment, I talked to my mother about Kelly and I moving out. She was not enthusiastic about the idea. This led to a period of internal turmoil for me. I began to act out, refusing to eat and often filled with anger. Despite my suffering, I couldn't bring myself to confide in anyone. I wanted to tell my mother, but a voice inside kept insisting that my sister's suffering was greater and that I needed to stay and support her. "Keep the dark secret to yourself," it whispered. "All will be fine. It will eventually go away."

Eventually, my mother relented, agreeing to our plan. We began our search for a new home and discovered a two-bedroom unit on the upper floor, accessible by a single door. I was overjoyed, convinced that God had answered my prayers. The new place felt like a safe haven, and I believed it would serve as a sanctuary for my sister, shielding her from her ex-husband. A few weeks later, we moved in. It was the happiest day of my life. We had found our freedom. Now, I had my own car and a place we could finally call home.

Kelly and I relished our newfound independence, frequently going out and having fun with a friend who lived downstairs with her two small children. While the kids stayed with their father, we enjoyed our freedom. My friend Helen often visited us with her young son, adding to the lively atmosphere. Other work friends would also drop by for coffee and conversation. Our place felt like a palace, furnished with everything we needed and brimming with warmth and peace.

A year later, Kelly and I set off on a two-week holiday to Fiji. We stayed at my parents' house, which rekindled old wounds, though I had buried them deep within. My father had arranged meetings with an Indian man he considered suitable for marriage. I met him but declined my father's suggestion. To my surprise, he accepted my decision, perhaps hoping to find someone else. During this trip, I reconnected with my school friends, who had completed their education and were now working, fulfilling a dream I shared. I felt no jealousy, as I was doing well in Australia. Catching up with everyone was wonderful, and my love for them remained strong. At my neighbour's house, I encountered someone I had liked back in primary school. We chatted for a while, and he gave me his address so we could stay in touch. Visiting all the family with my mum was a delight.

Upon returning home, our sanctuary felt like heaven. Resuming the rhythm of daily life, a letter arrived one day, bearing news from a friend from my primary school days. We embarked on a journey of correspondence, catching up on lost years and hoping to revive our bond. After months of exchanging letters and gradually understanding each other, another letter arrived in May, announcing his departure to the United States. Soon after, mutual acquaintances relayed the unsettling news of his marriage. This revelation stirred a tumult of emotions—sadness, anger, and a profound sense of rejection. Yet, from this heartache emerged a resolute determination: to shield myself from any future pain, to fortify my heart against further anguish.

Coincidentally in the same month, I received a letter that filled me with excitement—it was an invitation to a citizenship ceremony. This momentous news deepened my burgeoning connection to my new homeland. The ceremony was scheduled for the evening, and I was accompanied by Kelly and the kids, who came to share in my joyous occasion. As I stood there, the certificate in my hands, I was overwhelmed with gratitude and pride at being accepted as a citizen of Australia. In that instant, I promised to dedicate myself to my new country, feeling a profound sense of belonging that transcended the mere piece of paper I held.

Chapter 7

Miracle – Higher Powers

In the quiet suburbia of Endeavour Hills, a friendship bloomed amidst the passing years. Helen, a steadfast companion since 1984, had become a beacon of faith in my life. For three years, she had whispered of Jesus, his forgiveness, his grace. And as the whispers grew louder, I found myself yearning to find him, to embrace the peace he promised.

Amidst the longing for spiritual peace, a weariness settled upon my heart. Men, with their fleeting affections and broken promises, had left me disillusioned and disheartened. I resolved then, standing upon my balcony, to seek refuge in the sanctuary of a convent. Yes, I thought,

I shall be Mother Teresa's helper. But in that moment of intense feeling, I couldn't comprehend the tangled emotions within my Hindu heart.

Days turned into weeks, and the impulse to become a nun faded into the background of my consciousness. Yet, the yearning to find Jesus remained, a quiet ember glowing within. It was Helen's strong faith that kindled the flame anew. I asked her one Sunday, "Can I come to your church to find Jesus?" Her answer, gentle and affirming, filled me with hope: "Of course, anyone can come to church."

And so it was, on a Sunday much like any other, that I found myself seated in the pews of the church in Endeavour Hills, Victoria, alongside Helen. As the service unfolded, my gaze fixed upon the crucifix, and in the solemnity of that moment, I felt a peace wash over me. It was as though a burden had been lifted, as though someone had reached into the depths of my soul and whispered, "You are forgiven."

But amidst the serenity of that sacred space, questions swirled within me. Who was this man upon the cross? What had led him to such a fate? I yearned to unravel the mysteries of his story, to understand the depth of his love and sacrifice.

For in truth, I knew little of Jesus beyond the tales of Christmas and the promise of presents. Growing up in

Fiji, Christmas had been a time of joy and merriment, yet tinged with longing as I watched other children receive gifts. Oh, how I had daydreamed of joining their ranks, of being one of the chosen few who found favour in the eyes of Santa Claus.

As the service ended, Helen turned to me, her eyes filled with quiet understanding. "What did you think?" she asked. And in that moment, as I gazed upon the crucifix once more, I knew the answer. "Can I come again?" I whispered. And with a smile, Helen replied, "You can come anytime you want."

From that day forward, my Sundays were dedicated to attending church, a commitment I kept to myself, viewing it as a sacred bond between God and me. My heart and soul started to feel lighter and I found my purpose in life. Welcomed by a group of gracious women, I found myself drawn deeper into the teachings of scripture. With a beaming smile, I eagerly embraced the opportunity to delve into the wisdom of Jesus, envisioning a future where I would follow in the footsteps of Mother Teresa as a nun.

In the coming weeks, I seamlessly transitioned from mass to classes, sensing a profound sense of miracle unfolding before me. Each lesson brought peace, as if an unseen force guided me, easing the burdens of my past. It was a magical convergence, a divine orchestration of events revealing God's intricate plan.

Despite my newfound spiritual clarity, my resolve faced an unexpected test when my coworker friend, Kerrie, persistently suggested I meet her brother Mick in July 1988. Initially, I declined, steadfast in my commitment to a life of devotion. Yet, after repeated invitations, I relented, agreeing to a dinner outing under the assurance of Kerrie's presence alongside her husband in October. Keeping my intentions concealed from my family, I confided only in Kelly.

The evening began with casual conversation over dinner, followed by a viewing of "Edward Scissorhands." Despite the film, I found myself unmoved. However, as we chatted and laughed afterward, at home having a cup of tea, a persistent thought lingered: I was participating mostly to keep Kerrie happy, not wanting to jeopardise our friendship. After a cup of tea and a friendly kiss on the cheek from Mick, I went to bed, slipping back into the routine of my daily life.

When I saw Kerrie the next time at work, she mentioned Mick would ask me out again. I was taken aback. Hadn't I already been on a date with him? It turned out she meant just the two of us this time. A week later, Mick called and invited me to a French restaurant. I knew nothing about French cuisine or proper table etiquette, but I agreed nonetheless, figuring I had nothing to lose.

Our weekends transformed into joyous escapades, brimming with laughter and adventure. We ventured to new destinations like Ballarat, Bendigo, Geelong, Wilsons Promontory, Mornington Peninsula, and the Dandenong mountains. Occasionally, my beloved nieces accompanied us, and I cherished their presence as if they were my own children. He introduced me to experiences beyond my wildest dreams, and with each passing day, I fell deeper in love with him.

Summoning all my courage, I confided in Mick about my past. I prayed for honesty, knowing that if he couldn't accept me for who I was, then perhaps it wasn't meant to be. To my relief, he responded with compassion, acknowledging the pain I had endured.

As the weeks passed, I was getting nervous about meeting Mick's parents, apprehensive about how they might perceive me being Indian. I knew the traditional expectation that parents often preferred their children to marry within the same nationality, which added to my anxiety. My dad, who was still living in Fiji, had expressed his wish for me to marry within our Indian community, and he hadn't taken the news of my relationship with Mick well when he found out from an uncle.

A few weeks later, the moment arrived when I finally met Mick's parents. To my relief and delight, they welcomed me warmly. Both of them exuded kindness from the moment I entered their home. We settled into the lounge and engaged in a heartfelt conversation about my life, passions, and how Mick and I had found each other. Mick's mother, in particular, was incredibly friendly and curious, eager to learn all about my background and experiences. Her warmth and genuine interest put me at ease, dispelling my earlier apprehensions about whether I would be accepted.

On Christmas evening, I stayed over at Mick's house, settling into a spare bedroom. It didn't feel appropriate to share a room just yet. The next morning, as I entered the lounge, I was greeted by a sight that overwhelmed me – a multitude of beautifully wrapped presents scattered across the floor. Mick gestured for me to sit down, and then handed me 21 gifts, one for each year of my life that had passed without such celebrations. I was stunned; nothing like this had ever happened to me before.

With a blend of shock and joy, I began unwrapping the presents one by one. Among them were colouring books and pencils, Barbie dolls, teddy bears, a skateboard, and even a large toy horse, which Mick's niece would later delight in whenever she visited. Each gift was thoughtful and filled with care, culminating with a gold heart locket that touched me deeply. Mick's gesture was straight out of a movie, and I couldn't help but be overwhelmed by the love he showed me.

Feeling the warmth and love from Mick and his family enveloping me, I was overcome with emotion. Mick's thoughtfulness and the effort he had put into making this Christmas unforgettable for me left me speechless. It was a moment that made me feel like a child in a candy store, experiencing a Christmas unlike any I had known before. From that year onward, every Christmas with Mick and his family was filled with magic and joy. This first Christmas together marked the beginning of a new tradition and a deeper bond with Mick, reminding me of the love and happiness I had found in his embrace.

In December, shortly after Christmas, Kelly and I embarked on a journey to Sydney to visit our extended family. We travelled with a friend who lived in a downstairs unit with her two beautiful children. Over time, she had become a close friend. Despite Mick's fears of losing me, I reassured him that my heart remained steadfast, promising to keep him informed of my safety. This memorable trip, my first to Sydney, was filled with cherished moments among loved ones.

Returning home after a long journey, I was greeted by an unexpected sight: Mick waiting for me. Without hesitation, he asked for my hand in marriage. Overwhelmed with emotion, I said yes, my heart dancing with joy. In that moment, amidst the whirlwind of excitement, I couldn't help but wonder about the dreams of becoming a nun that had once occupied my thoughts. It all felt surreal, as if I were living in a dream.

A significant event loomed: my baptism. With Mick being Catholic, it seemed destined that I would embrace the faith as well. It felt like a miraculous turn of events, prompting me to wonder if some unseen hand was guiding our path. When Mick expressed his desire for a Catholic wedding, I eagerly agreed.

Tensions arose between Kelly and me, prompting me to move out and find my own place in February 1989. Mick had begun visiting in the evenings before work, but I couldn't shake the feeling that it was unfair to impose on Kelly and her children. Kelly had been my saviour, rescuing me from a past of abuse, and I was determined to ensure her safety and well-being. Despite the distance, I remained deeply attached to Kelly and her children, missing them dearly and cherishing the love we shared.

Living with Mick, who had slowly moved in with me, brought a sense of safety and comfort. His constant presence became an anchor in my life. However, beneath this surface of security, I grappled with conflicting emotions. On one hand, I felt a profound shame for not conforming to societal norms, on the other hand, this was just right for me. Living with a white man without being married left me feeling inadequate and fearful of judgment, especially from my parents. I knew they would never approve if they found out. Despite these doubts, I felt deep down that this was the right path for me, and I trusted in God to guide us. Continuing my weekly routine of attending church and delving deeper into scripture through classes after mass. Mick and I discussed our future together, exploring ideas about an engagement party, wedding plans, homeownership, starting a business, a holiday in Europe, and the possibility of starting a family. His foremost priority was to finish paying off the block of land he owned. Afterward, he planned to drive up to South Australia for a long weekend in June, marking my first trip to Adelaide. He was so dedicated to our goals that he even typed them out on an A4 sheet of paper. I still possess the original notes, and though we have accomplished every goal, it wasn't in the exact order we planned.

Despite finding peace in Mick's presence, an underlying anxiety gnawed at me. The fear of bringing shame upon my family weighed heavily on my conscience, and I couldn't shake the feeling that I was causing them distress. Despite my anger at the situation, I found strength in my faith and the supportive community at church. Mick's home provided a temporary respite from my anxieties, allowing me to feel a semblance of normality as I tended to everyday tasks. A few months later, Kerrie joyfully welcomed her first baby, a healthy boy. Mick and I were thrilled for Kerrie and her husband, eagerly anticipating the moment we could see and hold the baby. It was such a blessing to have another child in the family, especially since Mick's other sister, Dee, already had a two-year-old girl, the first grandchild.

I found peace in attending Saint Joseph's Parish, a church closer to my Chelsea unit, where I encountered a community of kind-hearted individuals. Immersing myself in scripture and fully engaging in classes, I found joy in the tradition of Sunday mass. The vibrant congregation of 1989, where latecomers often had to stand at the back. The Scottish priest, with his ever-present sense of humour, would always share a joke at the end of Mass, created a warm and welcoming atmosphere.

Our inaugural journey overseas whisked us away to Tahiti in August, a paradise where every moment felt like a dream. Amidst the breathtaking beauty that unfolded before me, I was struck by the realisation that such happiness was within reach. One perfect evening by the beach, I saw a shooting star and wished for peace and love. Beside me sat my beloved, whose presence made me feel safe. The moment was pure magic.

In September, we celebrated our engagement surrounded by loved ones in the hall. Despite the joyous occasion, my choice of a bright pink dress stirred unexpected emotions within me, stirring feelings of shame and guilt regarding my body. Doubts lingered, questioning my worthiness of such happiness. The shadow of the predator loomed, a grim reminder of a past I yearned to forget. Choosing silence, I buried the truth, convinced that revealing it would only lead to disbelief.

As life hurtled forward, news of my family's permanent residency to Australia stirred a familiar dread within me in October 1989. Faced with the prospect of protecting Bella, my younger sister, from the predator, I summoned the courage to confide in Mick, sharing the harrowing truth of my past. In his understanding embrace, I found peace, grateful for the release of my burdened heart.

I felt a swell of pride in Mick as he listened and reassured me, affirming that the fault lay squarely with the predator, not with me. In a bold move, Mick confronted the predator at his home, wielding a formidable stick as a warning against ever laying a hand on Bella. When I received a phone call at work from Mick asking me to come to my sister's house, I thought the predator was finally going to apologise for his crime. When I arrived, my two uncles, Mick, and the predator were standing outside. My sister was inside. I was shaking inside, hoping for a good outcome. All I remember was a lot of shouting, and then Mick and I got in our cars and went home.

Years later, when my sister and I resumed speaking, she confided in me that she had forgiven me for my mistake. I was taken aback—what mistake? While I had been struggling with the trauma inflicted by the predator, she had somehow forgiven me? She then disclosed that the predator had confessed to the incident but claimed that I had invited it. I couldn't believe my ears heard such lies - she believed him. I assured her it wasn't true. My love for my sister and my family ran so deep that I swallowed the hurtful words and buried them deep within.

Thankfully, Bella remained untouched, protected from harm by Mick's vigilance.

Chapter 8

God Sent

It was a difficult time, full of inner conflict. I wanted to tell my family about my suffering, but I couldn't bring myself to do it. Instead, I buried my feelings and acted like everything was fine. I believed my parents had suffered enough in Fiji and that my suffering would go away eventually. I hoped that in time, everyone would accept and love me.

Meanwhile, Mick and I envisioned our future together. Purchasing our first house in Frankston with Kerrie and her husband in February 1990 marked a significant milestone, albeit in an old house slated for demolition. Our dreams extended beyond Australia as we saved up for our first trip to Fiji. Helen, who joyfully welcomed her second child, a healthy baby girl, in February, asked Mick and me to be her godparents. Overwhelmed with disbelief, I felt profoundly honoured and grateful for the blessing. On the day of the baptism, Mick and I stood proudly beside Helen in the church, filled with a deep sense of pride and fulfillment.

As we embarked on the journey of planning, there was a significant milestone awaiting me beforehand – my baptism. Scheduled for Easter in April 1990, it filled me with anticipation. To be baptised and then wedded in the Catholic Church alongside Mick promised a transformative experience, akin to the rebirth I sought in Jesus, with Mick steadfastly by my side. Joining seven others in catechism classes, I eagerly prepared, adorning myself in a new outfit and cleverly decorated candle by Mick and a white garment sewed by my mum.

The decision to embrace Catholicism was deeply personal, a choice made for the betterment of my own soul. Each sacrament – reconciliation, baptism, confirmation – brought me closer to peace and fulfillment. As the water was poured on my head, I felt all my sins were forgiven. In the solemnity of the Mass, I felt a profound connection, fully immersed in the moment as I received the Eucharist for the first time, a transcendent experience that left me feeling blessed and renewed.

The support of the community buoyed me throughout this journey. The church overflowed with well-wishers on the day of my baptism, a testament to the love and encouragement that surrounded me. Following the ceremony, we gathered for a joyous celebration, complete with an impressive cake that seemed to symbolise the abundance of blessings in my life. Mick, ever the supportive partner, stood by me as my sponsor, guiding me through each step with constant devotion. Helen, my friend, beamed with pride, her support a beacon of encouragement amidst the celebration. She handed me a gift along with two handwritten prayers, "Our Father" and "Hail Mary," which I had to memorise. I was astonished to receive such thoughtful presents: a custom-made gold cross locket adorned with a small diamond from Mick's family and a gold locket of Mother Mary from Mick's grandmother, whom I had grown to love deeply. While my heart and soul were filled with pride at this milestone, my heart ached at the absence of my family during this once in a lifetime occasion. Their absence was a painful reminder of the rift caused by my choices. I felt guilty that their disappointment stemmed from my choice not only to marry outside of my culture but also to embrace a new religion. Despite this, I found comfort and wonderful support from Mick's family and my friends, their presence a reminder of the love and acceptance I had found in my new community.

The journey to Fiji in July was a transformative experience, surrounded by Mick's parents and his younger brother and the island's breathtaking beauty. As I stood amid this paradise, an overwhelming sense of gratitude mingled with guilt washed over me. Why did I deserve such happiness? Yet, amid these conflicting emotions, I rediscovered a profound love for my motherland. Each new experience felt like reclaiming my identity, a defiant stand against the shadows of past suffering. Despite the lingering scars of my history, I was determined not to let them overshadow the joy of the present. Exploring unfamiliar places and sharing moments with family and friends brought a renewed sense of excitement and fulfillment.

As we explored new vistas and forged deeper connections, I realised that my past no longer defined me. Instead, it served as a testament to my resilience and capacity for growth. Through embracing life's challenges, I discovered a newfound sense of purpose and belonging – a journey that led me to find peace and strength in unexpected places, ultimately transforming my suffering into a source of newfound resilience and joy.

Upon our return, we wasted no time in setting the date for our wedding: December 1990. I pressed on, determined to follow the path I had chosen, despite the obstacles and the silent disapproval that shadowed my happiness.

Chapter 9

True Wedding Vows

We chose to marry at Saint Joseph's Parish, the church where I had been baptised. The search for the perfect dress was next on the agenda. Accompanied by my mother-in-law and Kerrie, I headed to Melbourne city. It didn't take long to find a stunning white gown. Trying it on, I felt a surge of excitement, knowing our wedding would be a celebration of love. Everything about the process felt fresh, thrilling, and, most importantly, devoid of any shame or guilt. With joy, I asked my mum to craft the bridesmaids' dresses, and she eagerly agreed.

We encouraged my mum to come and stay with us in Frankston and attend TAFE to learn English. The school was within walking distance of our house. Mum was always a yes person, a quality I deeply admired. She absolutely loved learning English and soon improved. She made friends and enjoyed going to school.

Mum and I began reconnecting during this time, avoiding conversations about my past. Instead, we focused on planning my wedding and designing the dress together. It was a joyful period. My bridesmaids were Kerrie, Bella, and Helen. However, after Mum finished making the dresses, Helen had to withdraw from the wedding party because her husband disapproved. I was deeply disappointed; Helen was special to me because she introduced me to Jesus.

I chose Kerrie because she had persistently asked me to go out with her brother, and Bella because she encouraged me to speak my truth. With Helen no longer in the wedding party, I asked Kelly if she would like to be my bridesmaid, and she said yes. Although I felt bad about the situation, I realised Kelly had saved my life when she left her husband and now she was saving my bridesmaid dilemma. I couldn't thank her enough.

Mum had no trouble altering the dress for Kelly; she had a real knack for that kind of thing. Another dilemma arose when Dad hesitated to walk me down the aisle. He was unsure, and I didn't know how to reassure him. I had to convince him that everything would be fine and that he could do it. Finally, he agreed, and I felt a wave of relief.

Mick had his brother, my brother, and his uncle as groomsmen. Every detail needed to be organised months in advance: the venue, transportation, dinner, drinks, music, flowers, hotel arrangements, my parents' attire, the page boy and flower girl, rings, wedding vows, guest invitations, photographer, videographer, shoes, jewellery, wedding rehearsal classes, honeymoon plans, and so much more. We received a tremendous amount of support from family members, which made the planning process so much easier. I approached everything with excitement in my heart. It all felt so right—I was in love, and my life was improving day by day. I began feeling good about myself and thanked Jesus for all the blessings.

For our hen and buck's parties, Mick and I celebrated with family and friends at a theatre restaurant. It was an absolute blast.

The wedding day arrived with startling swiftness. Mick spent the night before the wedding at his parents' house, adhering to an old tradition. Meanwhile, I stayed at home with Kerrie, Kelly, and Bella. On the morning of the wedding, we prepared at Mick's aunt's house in Chelsea, conveniently close to the church. Our hair and makeup were meticulously done, and we all looked stunning. Surrounded by so much love, my heart was brimming with happiness, even as my stomach churned with nerves, uncertain about how everything would unfold at the church and the reception.

The bridesmaids dressed first, donning their long lemon-coloured gowns. They looked beautiful. As the preparations progressed, everything fell into place. My adorable little niece and the page boy seemed nervous, adding to the tender atmosphere. Finally, it was my turn to slip into my long white dress. Seeing myself in the mirror, I felt like a beautiful princess. Gratefully, I thanked Jesus for this incredible feeling. It felt like a dream, yet it was my reality.

When the horse and carriage arrived, I felt a childlike excitement at the prospect of sitting beside my dad on the ride to the church. A huge smile spread across my face as we set off. The afternoon was perfect for the leisurely journey to the church, and I savoured every moment. This was my special day, and I felt immense pride as my dad prepared to give me away in the church.

Walking down the aisle, I felt a whirlwind of emotions. First, the flower girl and page boy led the way, followed by my three bridesmaids. Finally, it was my turn. I caught my mum's eye and my mother-in-law's, exchanging heartfelt smiles. As I entered the church, filled with standing guests, my eyes found Mick, his groomsmen, and the priest. My life was on the verge of a profound transformation—soon I would be Mrs. Russell.

Mick and I exchanged our vows, a sacred moment marking the Fifth Sacrament, and sealed our promises with a kiss. It felt surreal. Just two years ago, I was on the path to becoming a nun, dedicating my life to serving others. Yet here I was, standing before my family and friends, feeling a higher presence enveloping us with love.

We signed the marriage register with the priest, my maid of honour, and the best man as witnesses. The ceremony was perfect, and my face ached from smiling so much for the photographer. But this was true joy—I had said yes. Outside the church, everyone enveloped us in hugs and congratulations. Yet, a tinge of sadness crept in as I noticed the absence of my elder sister and a few uncles. I had hoped everyone would share in my happiness.

The weather was perfect as the cart and horses carried us and the wedding party to the nearby reception. On the way, we stopped at a park for photos, laughing and enjoying every moment. The day was filled with love, joy, and blessings.

We arrived at the reception around 7 pm, where all the guests had gathered for drinks and snacks. The table setting looked lovely as we entered, following the wedding party. We were introduced as Mr. and Mrs. Russell, and everyone cheered and clapped. I felt incredibly special and supported in that magical moment as we settled in.

Then came a delightful surprise. A man dressed as a chimney sweeper, with a big broom, started dancing around. Everyone was taken aback but soon joined in laughter and applause. I found myself at the centre of attention as he approached, requesting a kiss on the cheek to an age-old English tradition, present from the in-laws signifying good luck and fertility on our wedding day. It was such a joyful experience; he continued to dance around the room, spreading laughter, and then left, leaving us all smiling.

After dinner, it was time for toasts and speeches. I felt immense pride as Mick stood up and said, "On behalf of my wife and me," thanking everyone for making our day so special. Then, my dad delivered a touching speech in both English and Hindi, expressing gratitude to all. His confidence speaking in public, despite initial reluctance to attend the wedding, made me especially proud. My parents, brother, and Bella had only been in Australia for just over a year, and today, my dad stepped out of his comfort zone. A strict Hindu deeply rooted in tradition gave his daughter away in a church to a white man; and she had converted to Catholicism.

Later, Mick and I had our first dance. I didn't know how to dance, but I moved around and enjoyed myself immensely. I didn't care; I was just so happy. The night seemed to pass too quickly, but as far as I was concerned, it was the best day of my life.

We were sent off to our hotel, and everyone was jubilant for us, singing, dancing, and embracing us. The next day, we departed for Singapore for our honeymoon, feeling deeply grateful to Jesus for sending me the love of my life.

Years later, when I heard the lyrics of Celine Dion's "Because You Loved Me," I realised that this song perfectly encapsulated my feelings for Mick.

Chapter 10

The Birth of a Motherhood

Surprisingly, three months after our wedding, I discovered I was pregnant. We had planned to start our family in two years. Nevertheless, we were so excited when we visited the doctor to confirm the news—we were going to have a baby. Both our families shared in our joy, their happiness radiating around us. Yet, amidst the celebration, memories of past pain and suffering surged back into my mind, casting a shadow over my newfound joy. An uneasy feeling settled within me, a persistent fear that something bad might happen. Desperately, I prayed for the health and well-being of my unborn child. Determined to give this baby the best start in life, I meticulously followed every guideline and took every precaution.

Each ultrasound brought fresh waves of emotions, seeing the tiny form of life growing inside me. The first kicks were magical, a gentle reminder of the life within, making the connection even more real.

Kerrie and I were pregnant at the same time, which gave me the confidence to lean on her, especially since she already had a two-year-old son.

I continued working throughout my pregnancy, feeling slightly unwell in the mornings for about two months. Other than that, I felt healthy. At seven months, I had to stop working because of company policy. Once I finished work, I practiced tai chi twice a week and walked twice a week to maintain my health.

The night before my due date, my mum stayed with me as Mick was working the night shift. When my water broke, Mick drove 160 kilometres per hour to reach me by 4:50 a.m. to take me to the hospital. I got in the car immediately, and we arrived at Frankston Hospital at 5:00 a.m. Two nurses greeted us at the door, and while Mick went to park the car, they supported me and laid me down in the first preparation room. The baby was already coming out.

THE BIRTH OF A MOTHERHOOD

Our daughter was born at 5:05 a.m. on Saturday, just moments after we arrived, and Mick missed the birth. Years later, he confessed he was having a cigarette. I went into shock, my body trembling. I remember the nurse saying, "It's a girl." My healthy, beautiful baby was crying and had to be cleaned up, so did I as we didn't make it to the labour room.

Holding my precious daughter in my arms, joy filled my heart. It was a miracle I could hardly believe had happened to me. Feeling immensely blessed; I whispered a prayer of thanks to Jesus for this incredible gift of life. Mick was by my side, tending to me with love and care, his pride in our family shining through his eyes.

In a moment of profound gratitude, I gave my daughter the middle name Teresa, in honour of Mother Teresa. Soon, the hospital room was filled with loved ones, each bringing gifts for the baby. The joy of seeing everyone together, celebrating this new life, made my heart swell with happiness. The sleepless nights that followed were challenging, but every smile, every coo, made it all worth it.

Ten days later, another blessing arrived when Kerrie welcomed her baby girl Emily into the world. Although she was expected to deliver before me, fate had its own plan, and we both welcomed healthy babies. It was a moment of pure joy and shared celebration.

Motherhood became my greatest motivator, igniting a fierce determination within me. I promised no one would ever hurt my baby.

The baptism of Teresa and Emily was a joyous occasion at St. Joseph's Parish, a place of profound significance for our family, where I was baptised and where we exchanged our vows. On this beautiful Australia Day in January, we gathered to celebrate together. The festivities continued with a lively gathering at Kerrie's house, overflowing with gifts and delectable food. Kerrie and I felt truly blessed, holding our precious bundles of joy in our arms, surrounded by love and happiness. Despite the celebration, I felt a deep ache for my absent family.

When Teresa was just three months old, I enrolled her in swimming lessons, determined to ensure she wouldn't inherit my fear of water. To my delight, the facility also offered adult swimming classes. Summoning all my courage, I confronted my own fears and signed up for lessons. My fear of water was so intense that I couldn't even bring myself to put my face under the surface. After a few lessons, I discovered a newfound sense of safety in the water and realised that I wasn't going to drown.

Unfortunately, after five precious months, I had to return to work. Kerrie offered to look after Teresa. I was immensely grateful for her offer, especially since my mother and I had become estranged once more. The ache of being separated from Teresa was a constant challenge, but Kerrie excelled in caring for both Teresa and her own children. I couldn't help but wish I could be the one looking after my little girl. Over time, Teresa and Emily grew to be inseparable, like twins.

As the days passed, I slowly came to accept that working was essential for our future. Our love for travel spurred me on, giving me the motivation I needed to keep going. Though it was challenging, I found comfort in knowing Teresa was in good hands.

In the serene setting of a park, we celebrated Teresa and Emily's first birthday, surrounded by family and friends. Watching the girls grow together brought immense joy to all of us. During this period, Mum began taking care of Teresa, which deepened our family bonds. I would call Mum every day from work to check on Teresa, feeling the ache of missing her deeply. Teresa started learning Hindi from my parents, and her visits there brought them a lot of joy.

Mick and I were invited to my cousin's Indian wedding, and I felt an overwhelming sense of joy for her, knowing she had found true happiness. However, a dilemma soon overshadowed my excitement: what was I going to wear? The thought of wearing a colourful sari and adorning myself with extravagant jewellery, like the rest of the guests, crossed my mind. But I quickly dismissed it as I felt I wasn't worthy of dressing up in Indian clothing.

The internal struggle was intense, and after much contemplation, Mick and I found a beautiful dress instead. We ventured to Chapel Street, where we discovered the most exquisite dress. It was unique and quite expensive, but it made me feel like a princess. Despite my stunning attire, as I stood among the women in their vibrant sarees and sparkling jewellery, a pang of longing struck me. Why couldn't I wear a sari like them?

Our first overseas trip with Teresa was to the Cook Islands and Western Samoa when she was just eighteen months old. We had an amazing time together. The people in Western Samoa were especially welcoming, often taking Teresa into the kitchen to feed and adore her. Mick got a bit concerned when she didn't come back after a few minutes, but I reassured him that no harm would come to Teresa; the locals were incredibly friendly and loving.

The Cook Islands were equally enchanting. We commissioned a local artist to create a painting for us, choosing a vibrant and colourful subject. To our surprise and delight, she included an image of a future son in the painting, even though having more children was not on our minds. I treasure this painting deeply; it still hangs in my home, and I look at it every day with fond memories.

For six months, while our unit was getting built alongside Kerrie's, we slept in a caravan in my in-law's driveway, a time that allowed me to forge a deeper connection with my mother-in-law. She had an uncanny ability to understand my pain, and this empathy created a bond between us. Our stay there was filled with warmth and joy.

Life was busy with work and family. When I heard Kelly was getting married again, my heart leapt with joy. Finally, she would experience the same happiness that I had found. Determined not to miss this joyous occasion, I made sure to be there. The wedding was a small, intimate Hindu ceremony held at home, surrounded by close family and friends. I felt incredibly grateful for the chance to witness this special moment. Being there with Teresa, enveloped by the warmth of our family, made the day even more special. When I offered Kelly a full-time position at my workplace, she eagerly accepted. Soon, she was working full-time and earning her own money. I felt immense happiness for Kelly, knowing she had always been a diligent worker. Each interaction with her at work brought me joy.

The excitement of moving into our brand-new unit was palpable. We had eagerly purchased all new furniture, ready to create a fresh and inviting space. I absolutely adored our cosy three-bedroom unit. The joy of settling in was doubled by the fact that Kerrie and her family were our new neighbours, making it a true celebration.

When our daughter was just three years old, we embarked on our family trip to Asia, visiting Thailand, Hong Kong, and Singapore. Everywhere we went, people were incredibly friendly and adored our little one. Mick and I fell in love with Thai food and culture, savouring every bite and soaking in each unique experience. One sunny afternoon, I took Teresa to the pool for some leisure time. As she joyfully splashed near Mick, I took a swim myself. My enjoyment was short-lived as I soon found myself in the deep end, gripped by panic and crying out for help. Mick swiftly came to my rescue, pulling me to safety. This harrowing experience left me with a lasting fear of deep waters and a respect for their power.

One Christmas morning, Mick surprised me with the biggest present I had ever seen. For an entire week, he had been teasing me about how much I was going to love my gift, and the anticipation had left me feeling increasingly nervous. When he finally unveiled the present, my anxiety peaked. It was a bicycle, and I had never ridden one before.

Faced with the challenge, I knew I had no choice but to learn. I began practicing in our long driveway, and gradually, my confidence grew. Eventually, Mick and I ventured out onto the road. It was terrifying at first, but with each ride, my fear diminished, and I discovered the thrill of cycling.

Immediately after Christmas, Kerrie and I embarked on a mission to plan a surprise party for Mick. With Mick occupied at work, Kerrie would come over, and we would sit together, planning and organising until 2 AM.

We meticulously arranged every detail, ensuring Mick remained blissfully unaware. On the day of the party, we pretended we were heading out for dinner. We mentioned a necessary stop to pick up Mick's brother at the hall. As Mick stepped inside to get his brother, he was greeted by a room filled with loved ones. The surprise was complete; Mick was astonished that we had kept such a secret from him. The night unfolded beautifully, with music, dance, and the warmth of family and friends.

Our journey to Fiji with Teresa, who was just three and a half years old, was an adventure we'll never forget. It was a time of reunion with family and friends as we explored the island together. Visiting Vanua Levu, the second largest island, for the first time was a particularly profound experience for me. I felt an overwhelming sense of peace and a deep connection to my motherland. As we prepared for this holiday, the thought of having a second child was already on our minds.

Amidst the whirlwind of everyday life, a joyful event was on the horizon for our family—a grand celebration was in the works. My only brother was set to marry in a few months, and the news filled me with excitement. However, a familiar dilemma soon crept in: what would I wear? After weeks of contemplation, I concluded a sari was out of the question. It didn't feel right; I felt unworthy. My yearning to belong within my family was intense, and I longed to voice my truth, to explain the reasons I had distanced myself—hoping for their understanding and love, much like Mick had given me. I believed that this love could soothe my wounds. Deep down, my soul reassured me I was on the right path, but my mind still craved acceptance from my family. I missed them terribly.

Weeks after the wedding, we received the life-changing news we had been waiting for over six months—I was pregnant. Mornings now greeted me with waves of nausea, yet they were intertwined with joy, excitement, and a touch of nervousness. Questions swirled in my mind: How would I love this baby? Would I have enough love for everyone? Thankfully, I found that my capacity for love was boundless.

By the fourth month, my health necessitated a bittersweet decision to leave work, opening the opportunity to reconnect deeply with Teresa. We dove into swimming lessons, kindergarten activities, and countless moments of fun. This precious time together was made even more special by living next to Kerrie and the kids, allowing us to fully embrace and cherish our close-knit community.

Four and a half years later, on a cold Saturday morning at 6.28 a.m. in June, we welcomed our second child into the world. This time, the experience was different, but equally miraculous. Having gone through it once before, I felt more prepared, but the anticipation was just as high. When our beautiful boy, Luke, arrived, the intensity and extraordinariness of the moment took my breath away. Labour was long and arduous, but the instant I heard his first cry, my world shifted. Holding him for the first time, feeling his tiny heartbeat against my chest, I was overwhelmed by a love so profound it brought tears to my eyes. Once again, I was awestruck by the miracle of life.

The sleepless nights that followed were challenging. Luke, a hefty 9-pound baby, couldn't be fully satisfied with breastfeeding alone. Carrying such a big baby while pregnant had taken a toll on my back, leaving me sore and exhausted. These were trying times for my body, and I quickly realised I needed to prioritise my health to care for my precious children. The doctor advised me to rest and avoid lifting Luke, which brought me to tears, though I knew it was impractical. Thankfully, with the help from Mick and Kerrie, I got by. Some laser treatment on my back provided relief from the pain. Teresa was captivated by her baby brother, and witnessing their bond develop became one of the greatest joys of my life. During the time I was grappling with the challenges of caring for my newborn, my brother and his wife joyfully welcomed their own baby boy just two months later. The happiness I felt was immense, especially for my parents, who were proud grandparents, affectionately called Aja and Aji.

On a beautiful, sunny September day, as the first signs of spring blossomed, we gathered at St. Francis Parish in Frankston, our cherished local church, to celebrate Luke's baptism. The celebration carried on in a rented hall, alive with the warmth of family and friends and the enticing aromas of catered food. My heart overflowed with joy as I watched everyone bring presents for my baby and offer their heartfelt well-wishes. The sight of all the cousins playing together, their laughter filling the air, was truly heartwarming, especially a newly born cousin. I felt profoundly blessed on this special day.

Life became a whirlwind of activity, filled with feeds, nappy changes, baths, school runs, homework, and preparing healthy dinners. Mick's night shifts added to the challenge, and I worked hard to ensure the baby didn't cry for too long, mindful of his need for rest. I found joy in volunteering at Teresa's school, helping with reading and other activities, which I loved and at the same time making new friends.

When Luke was only five months old, Mick's sister Dee approached me with a captivating business idea. She suggested we start a venture together, showcasing my exquisite Indian cuisine at various markets, events, and festivals. Enthusiastic yet resolute, I agreed on one condition: while I was more than happy to prepare the food, I would not be the one selling it. I couldn't bear the thought of facing the public, fearing they might see the pain I was hiding inside. And so, Gyan's Curry House was born.

THE BIRTH OF A MOTHERHOOD

Before the launch of our business, we embarked on a delightful trip to Mildura with Kelly and her family, along with Bella and Mum. We rented a minibus, allowing us to travel together comfortably. Our days were filled with joy as we attended wine and jazz festivals, picked fresh oranges straight from the trees, enjoyed dinners out, and took leisurely rides on the boat. I felt so blessed and proud of my achievement, which included my loving husband, my two healthy children—a girl and a boy—and the rest of the family with me, hoping all my pain would disappear into the woods. I felt so much love around me.

As our venture progressed, my sister-in-law had to step away from the business because of her pregnancy. Mick and I resolved to elevate the business. We soon realised that managing a business and raising two children in our small unit was increasingly challenging due to space constraints. Reluctantly, we decided to rent out our beloved unit. Concurrently, Kerrie had sold her unit and was in the process of building a new house. In no time, we discovered the perfect house to accommodate our expanding family and business needs.

In June, on a freezing cold evening, we celebrated Luke's first birthday in our new house. We invited all our family and friends, combining the joy of Luke's special day with the excitement of unveiling our new home. The open fire blazed warmly, warding off the chill, while everyone indulged in an abundance of delicious food.

Three weeks later, we joyfully welcomed another addition to our family—a baby boy, Dee's bundle of joy. I felt immense gratitude for Dee and her innovative business plan, which had brought us all together in this special moment. Everything was going smoothly until Luke was 15 months old, when I discovered I was pregnant again. The news, though unexpected, filled us with joy. However, our happiness was short-lived. At three months, I suffered a miscarriage. The loss was devastating. I blamed myself, convinced I hadn't taken proper care of my body. Sadness engulfed me, and I often found myself tearing up while driving. I buried my feelings deep inside, focusing on the business and constantly reminding myself that I already had two healthy children—why would I need more? While Mick continued working shift work during the week, he dedicated his weekends to assisting me with our growing business. Starting with small events, we gradually expanded, taking on larger events like the Melbourne Cup, the air show, the motorcycle Grand Prix at Phillip Island, craft markets in Victoria, and various wine and food festivals. As our business flourished, we began employing family members, arranging their shifts to evenly distribute the workload. Our two children were cared for by different family members, taking turns as needed.

As each larger event came and went, the demand for food grew. I took on the responsibility of purchasing, preparing, and cooking all the food myself. Working from home, I felt incredibly privileged to be able to drop Teresa off at school every morning and pick her up in the evening. Being involved in all her school activities was something I cherished deeply.

On Sundays, when there were no events, I took my family to church. This brought me a great deal of peace, sitting for an hour in meditation and prayers, surrendering all my pain to Jesus. I believed that praying as a community made the prayers stronger. I loved my church community, where I could be myself without judgment.

Every Tuesday, while Teresa was at school, Luke, my mum, and I would head to the market to buy fresh food and vegetables. This experience allowed my mum and I to reconnect, creating wonderful memories together. She always had some delicious food for me at lunch, which I eagerly anticipated. Often, I would run late to pick Teresa up because of the 25-minute drive.

On cooking days, I still spent quality time with Luke, which I treasured. One of my most cherished memories is resting on the couch after finishing my cooking, with Luke snuggling up next to me and falling asleep. These moments were incredibly precious to me.

Mick dedicated every spare moment to building a mobile kitchen. No longer would we need to set up a white marquee or deal with the aftermath of a rainy event—or so we hoped. Before long, we scheduled two events on the same weekend. It might sound crazy, and it was. Mick would head to one event with the mobile kitchen and some family members, while I attended another with a different set of relatives. Together, we traversed Victoria, and in Geelong, I witnessed the Dalai Lama spreading love and peace to thousands of people. The energy was incredible, and serving our delicious food to eager customers was exhilarating. Despite the challenges of work and travel, I loved every moment. I visited amazing places and met wonderful people, making every effort worthwhile.

Mick and I always made our holidays a top priority. We took Luke to Fiji for the first time when he was just two years old. Our stay was split into two parts: one week at a luxurious resort and the second week with my cousin. It was an incredibly fun and memorable trip. Having Teresa and Luke with us made me feel complete. Every time we went away, Mick and I felt a stronger connection, as he was more relaxed, free from the stresses of work and home. For me, holidays were about savouring the moment with my family and not entertaining the pain within.

When I heard Bella was getting married, after we returned from our holidays, I couldn't have been happier. She had once refused to marry, even when everything was already organised. I admired Bella's courage. However, the week of the wedding, I came down with shingles. I wasn't sure if I'd be able to attend. My face was covered in large spots, and I felt so sick that all I wanted to do was sleep. I didn't have time to think about what to wear, so I ended up wearing a dress again. I covered my face with layers of makeup and managed to look presentable. Upon my arrival, the sight of everyone in their stunning saris made my heart ache with a longing to belong. My Bella looked breathtaking in the red and yellow sari with exquisite jewellery. My love for her swelled within me.

Business was thriving, and each week, I was forming strong connections with my mum. Now that mum didn't have any commitment, we invited her to join us on a trip to Thailand. The experience was unforgettable. Every day, after exploring the sights, mum and I would unwind with soothing foot massages. Her easy-going nature made her adaptable to any situation, adding to the joy of our trip. When I heard Kelly was pregnant after over six years of marriage from mum when we were on our holiday, I quickly prayed for her and the baby. Fortunately, everything went smoothly, and in 2000, she welcomed a healthy baby girl—her third daughter. I was overjoyed for her and thrilled at the prospect of more cuddles.

Life had become incredibly busy with our mobile business, so much so that it was taking a toll on our home life. We decided it was time to open a shop and stop travelling all around Victoria. Meanwhile, Mick's workplace was shutting down, leaving him without a job. Together, we signed a three-year lease in a shopping centre.

Before diving into this new venture, we took a holiday to Cairns in Queensland. We were captivated by the beautiful, sunny weather, a stark contrast to Melbourne's. It was then that we decided we would move to Cairns once our three-year commitment to the shop ended.

Returning home, we established the shop, marking the beginning of a new chapter in our lives. While we continued operating our mobile business, we had to scale it back to focus on the shop. It was hard work, running the shop seven days a week while still managing the mobile catering. I found myself solely responsible for all the cooking, both for the shop and events, with a team of ten employees working for me.

Most of the time, I was lost in my thoughts, wishing for a baby. But I kept pushing the thought away, reminding myself I already had two beautiful children. At events, I asked to hold other people's babies, wondering if I was going mad. At other times, I thought it wouldn't be fair to get pregnant while running the shop. When Bella welcomed her bundle of joy in 2001, my heart overflowed with happiness. Another baby girl meant more cradles to rock and tiny hands to hold. I hoped that this new addition would quell my longing to have a baby of my own, but the feeling only grew stronger. After Bella returned to work, my mother took on the role of caring for my niece, and I connected with her every week. She accompanied us to the market, and I cherished those precious moments. I loved her dearly, and she brought me immense joy. Organising chores for the home, planning events, and managing the shop became increasingly overwhelming. Yet, these tasks kept me occupied, offering a welcome distraction from the aching desire for a baby of my own.

Mick orchestrated a truly unforgettable surprise for my 35th birthday. He had cleverly convinced me we were attending a prestigious sailing club ball, even insisting that I wear an elegant gown for the occasion. He even showed me a printed invitation, which he had meticulously arranged. To ensure everything ran smoothly, he organised for two ladies to cover the shop in our absence.

Upon our arrival at the club, where he held membership, I was utterly astonished to find all of our family and friends assembled inside. As I stepped into the centre of the room, a cascade of balloons descended, marking a moment of sheer joy and surprise. Every detail of the party was perfect, a testament to Mick's exceptional planning and his skill at maintaining the surprise. That night, I felt extraordinarily special. Helen, Kerrie, and I danced the night away, revelling in the joyous celebration.

Kerrie suggested hiring a housecleaner. Initially hesitant, I knew deep down that I needed help. When we finally hired one, she was amazing. Mick also had to hire someone to take care of the lawn as he was getting too busy with events and working in the shop. Our neighbour kindly looked after our children while I was at the shop, but I started feeling guilty for not being able to take care of them myself.

My shoulders ached from hours of preparing and cooking, a constant strain that mirrored the pain of my monthly periods. Each time, I was engulfed by waves of despair, plagued by suicidal thoughts. Guilt followed swiftly, as I thought of my children and felt the heavy weight of responsibility. My kids were the anchors that kept me tethered to life, reminding me of my duty to be there for them.

As the stress weighed heavily on me, I began staying home with the children while Mick managed the shop and the staff. One day, while Kelly was working in the shop with Mick, a misunderstanding arose concerning my niece. I intervened, trying to protect her, but it led to a disagreement with Kelly. As a result, Kelly and I didn't speak for the next 15 years. This rift made me question myself, wondering if I was the source of the family's troubles. The stress became unbearable, manifesting in physical symptoms. Red welts appeared on my back, hands, and stomach, covering my body and deepening my anxiety. A visit to the doctor confirmed my suspicions—an article in the waiting room highlighted the myriad ways stress can wreak havoc on the body. I realised that stress was the root of my suffering.

Determined to find relief, we planned a holiday, leaving the shop in the capable hands of the ladies who worked there. I invited my mother to join us, and she was thrilled. Our trip to Malaysia was transformative. With no business or house chores to worry about, I felt a lightness and happiness that had eluded me for so long. Being with my family nourished my spirit, and I knew brighter days lie ahead.

During that blissful escape, a stark revelation emerged: the shop had to go. What had once been a source of immense pride had transformed into a relentless burden. The realisation struck with undeniable clarity—I could no longer shoulder the weight of the business. For the past five years, I had been denying my soul's deepest yearning: the desire to have a baby.

As my stress levels soared, my physical pain intensified to where cooking became impossible. Mick had to take over the kitchen duties while I supervised from a seat. A visit to the doctor resulted in a prescription for antidepressants, and I broke down in tears. I knew I had to find another way to feel better because, deep down, I understood why I was feeling depressed.

The path to healing was only just beginning, but recognising the toll stress had taken on my body and mind was the first crucial step. I enrolled in a weekly yoga class while Luke was at kindergarten and Teresa was at school. Walking became a solace, allowing me to admire the beautiful gardens on my way to pick up my children. Sometimes, I paused at the park, creating games for the kids using the equipment. I needed to be strong for them. I attended every activity at school, church, and kindergarten. Both children took swimming lessons—Teresa joined a netball team, and Luke joined a basketball team. They both took piano lessons, and I made sure I was present and attentive. Keeping my kids safe became my priority. Mick and I ensured we were there for every training and game session. Amidst the bustle of school life, Teresa's confirmation party at home, surrounded by family and friends, was a highlight, especially with my dad attending. I felt immense pride when Teresa spoke confidently in front of a church full of parents and kids at a Christmas nativity play, a feat I had always struggled with. I was invited to serve my food at a multicultural event at the school, which I loved because it meant more people tasting my food. I knew all the school staff and admired their amazing work.

I vowed to bring my children to every family gathering, determined to immerse them in our vibrant culture and remind them of their Indian heritage. Teresa, especially, delighted in these occasions, cherishing the chance to wear exquisite Indian outfits.

When it came time for high school, Mick and I searched extensively for a good Catholic school for Teresa. We eventually found one in Belgrave, nestled in the Dandenong mountains, Mater Christe. In 2003, Teresa started high school there. Every morning, I would drive her ten minutes to a bus stop, from where she would catch a school bus for a one-hour ride to her school. I found this arrangement less than ideal, as the distance seemed too great. Fortunately, we didn't have to continue this routine for long.

During this period, I kept the shop running with the assistance of the charming ladies, while Mick secured a full-time job. The shop was put up for sale, and by October, it was sold, bringing me a sense of profound relief. With the shop no longer a concern, I concentrated exclusively on two profitable markets. On market days, Mick would lend a hand, Teresa took on the role of serving the customers, and Luke would entertain himself by making friends with the children of other stall holders.

The first thing we did was book a holiday to Fiji. Mick and I desperately needed this time with our children. I had missed them so much, having been so busy and silently suffering. This time, I resolved not to entertain my pain. I whispered to myself, "You can wait. I am on holiday." We had an amazing time together. I felt a deep happiness within me, as if my soul had been yearning for this moment.

After the shop was sold, we sold our house and moved closer to Teresa's school. We took a holiday to Tasmania and I asked my mum to join us once again, and she was thrilled. We traveled all around Tasmania, marvelling at the beautiful scenery. Once again, I connected deeply with Mum. She loved spending time with the children, and we did many fun activities, travelling around in a car we took over on the ferry. I felt truly happy inside.

Our house sold quickly, and to our immense joy, I discovered I was pregnant, something I had longed for so long. Everything was moving so quickly that we didn't have a moment to waste. We found a place to rent in Selby while we searched for a house to buy. I continued working at the two markets and hired a lady to help with cooking, which made things easier during my pregnancy.

I got involved in the new school activities and the parish, quickly making friends. We enjoyed going out for lunch and each other's company. Luke settled in well at school and made good friends. A couple of months later, winter hit hard, with the cold seeping into my bones. We moved to a warmer climate, Cairns like we promised ourselves, encouraged by our family who already visited Townsville who assured us it was a great place to raise kids.

In October, we visited Townsville, eager to see if it might be the right place for us. From the moment we arrived, we fell in love with the town. It had everything we needed and seemed perfect for raising children. Just a 20-minute boat ride away was Magnetic Island, offering the perfect quick getaway.

THE BIRTH OF A MOTHERHOOD

The highlight of our trip was our adventure on the Great Barrier Reef. After two hours on the ferry, Teresa and several others were vomiting, and most of us felt nauseous. Thankfully, once we arrived and stopped, everyone felt better. Mick and Teresa went scuba diving while Luke and I opted for the glass-bottom boat. It was a wonderful experience, being under the water and marvelling at the marine life below.

Soon after, we all went snorkelling. I was amazed by the natural beauty surrounding me. At one moment, I felt a sense of magic, only to be quickly replaced by fear when I realised where I was. I screamed for help, and Mick swiftly came to my rescue, guiding me back to the ferry. I think being six months pregnant gave me the courage to venture into the open ocean, despite the initial fear.

Upon returning home, I began the hardest task of selling all my market equipment, mobile kitchen, cars, and any extra belongings we didn't need. Each sale was a step towards our impending move to Townsville, and though the process was often challenging, I remained focused on the goal. Letting go of these pieces of our past was difficult, but it was a necessary part of our journey.

One day while I was at home packing, my phone rang. It was my niece, calling to tell me she was coming over for a visit. Her call took me by surprise; it had been a year since she had invited me to her wedding, an event I had chosen not to attend. The decision had left my heart aching for weeks, as she was my favourite niece, but her mum and I were not talking.

During our conversation, she delivered shocking news: the predator was at his games again. My vision blurred with rage upon hearing this. Desperate for confirmation, I called my mum. She confirmed the devastating truth.

I thought to myself despite Mick's intervention all those years ago, the predator didn't care about anyone but himself. My heart weighed heavily with guilt. I couldn't shake the feeling that I had failed to protect others. I should have spoken up, done more, gone to the police, done something - anything. But who would have believed me anyway?

Our move to Townsville was drawing near, a time that should have been joyful, but instead, it only deepened the rift with my mum, and I ended up screaming at my sister again, and I disconnected with her for the next ten years.

I was heartbroken for my niece. This disconnect between Kelly and I had kept me in the dark about everything. The very reason I had distanced myself in the first place was to protect her daughter from harm. Despite my efforts to reach out and support my niece, I ended up interfering once more, which only angered my mum further. She had vowed to be in Townsville when I gave birth, but she never came. Her absence devastated me. I endured the pain in silence, longing for my mother's presence, waiting in vain for the call that would bring me to the airport to pick her up.

The calls from my dad became a lifeline. He checked on me regularly, showing me the constant love and support I desperately needed. He couldn't understand why my mum was so angry with me, and his confusion mirrored my own. I felt like I was causing trouble all over again.

As time passed, I came to understand that my mother couldn't bear the weight of my truth. She, too, was tormented by her own inner struggles - losing a daughter to suicide then three years later a daughter was raped by someone she trusted. All this must have been overwhelming, leaving her unable to offer the support I needed. Living in a predator's house, it was simpler to remain silent, to avoid resurrecting the past and to let it stay buried.

Motherhood is not without its trials. There were moments of doubt and exhaustion, times when I questioned if I was doing it right. But through it all, the bond with my children grew stronger. They taught me patience, resilience, and the true meaning of unconditional love. More importantly, they taught me how to be more protective. In hindsight, this could have been my beacon for finding my voice to face the predator.

Chapter 11

Townsville & Travelling

We arrived in Townsville on December 4, 2004, under the relentless blaze of an exceptionally hot day. I was eight months pregnant, and the heat seemed even more oppressive because of it. Swimming helped, but often I stayed indoors with the air conditioning as walking became increasingly difficult.

We stayed for over two and a half weeks in a modest rental unit while searching for a more permanent residence. On December 22, we moved into a grand, beautiful Queenslander with a swimming pool. It felt like a perfect new beginning.

We celebrated Christmas Day at the RSL restaurant, where we indulged in an abundance of food and drinks. We had a wonderful time, though we missed our families dearly.

On Saturday morning, while the rest of the household was still sleeping, I rose early to pack away the Christmas tree and decorations and tidy up the house. I had a premonition that our baby would be arriving that day. As lunchtime approached, the unmistakable pains of labour began. With no friends or family in town to assist, we had no choice but to bring Teresa and Luke with us to the hospital.

At precisely 4:40 p.m., our baby boy, Xavier, entered the world, joining his siblings in the tradition of being born on a Saturday. The delivery went smoothly, and our hearts overflowed with joy as we welcomed another miracle into our lives. I requested the nurse to place Xavier on my chest, savouring the long-awaited moment and offering thanks to Jesus for this precious bundle of joy.

During this time, my only visitors were my children and Mick. I asked the nurse if I could extend my hospital stay for a few more days to aid in my recovery. Fortunately, it was a school holiday, so the kids were available to help. Teresa, ever the little mother, was incredibly helpful, and Luke was thrilled to have a baby brother. Mick found a job a couple of weeks later working shift work, and the kids started school. We chose schools close to each other so Luke could walk to Teresa's school and wait for me there.

On the first day I dropped Luke off at St Joseph's school, a group of ladies invited me for coffee right after the assembly. I instantly connected with them, and it became a regular occurrence. A few of them are still my best friends. Sometimes, we would go out for lunch with the baby, finding a quiet corner to breastfeed Xavier on demand. There were always enough lovely ladies around to cuddle Xavier. On other days, I would drop the kids off at school and walk the entire length of the Strand. I even started volunteering in the classroom, helping with reading while Xavier sat contentedly in his pram.

In the narrative of my life, my mother-in-law, whom I tenderly refer to as my second mum, emerged as a beacon of hope and salvation. During some of my most harrowing moments, she graciously stepped in to offer her kind support. Her frequent calls, sometimes three times a day, served as lifelines, Ensuring that my family and I were managing. She resonated deeply with my pain, having navigated through tough times with her own family. For her compassion and understanding, I am immensely grateful to Jesus for blessing me with my second mum.

When I heard that the family was organising a surprise party for her 60th birthday in early March, I knew I had to attend with her three grandkids. I also wanted to introduce our newborn baby to everyone. Unfortunately, Mick couldn't join us as he was working. Despite his absence, we had an amazing celebration for my second mum. She was genuinely surprised, and I was overjoyed to be there, especially with her youngest grandchild.

A few days later, I was visiting my uncle and aunt. My mum was staying with them for a short while. We were sitting and having a conversation when the predator walked in. It felt as if Jesus had sent him so I could finally speak my truth. An ugly rage bubbled up inside me, and I vomited it all out in front of my kids. I needed to express my truth in front of my mum, uncle, and aunt. There was no time to think; I just saw red and lost control of my words and my body. I forgot where I was, my body shaking as I finished speaking and shouting at him. I remember shouting out at him he should have known better. I was only 17, and he took advantage of me and lied about it to his wife. I don't really remember half of the things I said.

After that, I picked up my baby, Teresa, grabbed the bag, and I told Luke to get in the car. The predator came outside with everyone and threatened to smash the car as he started looking for a weapon. My mum told him it wasn't my car. I quickly got away, my body still shaking and my mind raging with anger. I thought I had found my voice in front of my mum, aunt, and uncle to say what was in my heart. Yet speaking my truth in that moment seemed to change nothing; I only frightened my children.

Once more, I found no peace. Instead, I buried my anger and frustration deep within, adding it to the growing reservoir of pain.

Upon our return from Melbourne, Teresa and I eagerly joined the local netball club. My passion for the game made it a delightful experience, especially since I had the pleasure of playing alongside Teresa. We shared countless laughs, and the team spirit grew even stronger when the other ladies endearingly nicknamed me "G" due to their struggle with pronouncing my first name. Meanwhile, Luke became a member of the soccer club, and both kids continued with their piano lessons. Luke also persevered with his swimming lessons.

Sadly, after one fun season, I had to quit playing netball because of a knee injury. The risk of making it worse was too great, especially since I had no backup support for my kids. Teresa kept playing and even made it onto a team that would travel to Adelaide to represent her club from Townsville. While I didn't want her to go because I worried about her, I also wanted her to experience life, and she was so excited to make the team. I missed the camaraderie with the ladies and the thrill of the game deeply. One bright spot from that time was receiving my first-ever trophy—a cherished reminder of my brief but joyful time with the netball club.

Weeks later, during a conversation with mum, when I mentioned the predator, she remarked I was causing trouble everywhere I went. From that day, I promised myself never to speak my truth again, and I believed her statement. I started believing that it was me who was causing the problem. My heart shattered into pieces; I don't know how I put my heart back together. I suppose I didn't have a choice. The kids kept me busy, and I needed to be present for them. I suffered silently, keeping my pain to myself while continuing with life. I often wondered what the predator must have told my mum on the way home as my parents were staying at his house. I kept myself busy with house chores and taking Xavier to swimming lessons during the day. After school, I juggled various activities and started planning for Xavier's baptism and Luke's ninth birthday, both set to take place during the June school holidays. My favourite aunt, the first to arrive from Sydney, was an enormous help in organising Luke's party. I invited several of his school friends and football teammates and their parents. Everyone had an incredible time. Mick cooked naan bread, and I cooked butter chicken for the parents while the kids had party food.

Our home was filled with life as we welcomed nine visitors from Melbourne, a mix of family and friends who brought a joyful energy to the house. Kerrie arrived with her two kids, and Helen with her daughter. My in-laws joined us as well, along with two other friends. The house was full, buzzing with endless conversations. It was the kind of gathering I usually loved, the kind that filled every corner with light and noise. Yet, amidst the joy, a quiet truth weighed heavily on my heart: none of my family had been invited. Once again, I had distanced myself, feeling the familiar sting of heartache but burying it deep within, hidden beneath the surface of my smile.

Xavier's baptism at St. Joseph's, alongside two other families, was a beautiful ceremony. Afterward, we had a celebration at home and enjoyed each other's company. We even made a trip up to Mission Beach. Some of the visitors ventured to Cairns, while others went to Bowen, and we came home. The most enjoyable day was at Magnetic Island, a quick ride on the ferry. It was a time filled with joy and the creation of wonderful memories.

Six months after his 40th birthday, Mick decided it was time for a career change. He enrolled in a drafting course at TAFE, taking classes at night after work. Mick had always been eager to learn new things, and this was no different. Once he completed the six-month course, he quickly landed a job as a draftsman, marking his third job in just 18 months.

As the netball season ended, we packed up once more, with the house now on the market. Our new home, just a five-minute drive away, was a cosy single-story house with a small swimming pool. I spent a lot of time in the pool, working to overcome my fear of water while the kids were at school. The entire family joined me in riding bikes, helping me build my confidence. I relished the sense of freedom that came with it.

After dropping the kids off at school, I began delivering advertising materials into letter boxes a few times a week. Occasionally, the kids would help after school, adding a bit of family teamwork to the task. This, combined with the usual housework, kept me quite busy.

Mick came up with a great idea one day—he wanted his niece to attend a Catholic high school, believing it would give her a better start in life. He was always thinking of ways to help others and wanted to see everyone succeed, so he paid her school fees. I agreed wholeheartedly. Unfortunately, we didn't pay for the entire duration, as her mum eventually took over the fees. She went on to university, earned a degree in Education, and now teaches at a high school. Mick and I couldn't be prouder of what she has accomplished.

Life seemed to flow beautifully when Mick and I embarked on our dancing lessons. My desire to learn to dance properly led us into this new adventure. While Teresa and Luke kept a watchful eye on their baby brother, I found myself challenged by the steps. Despite the difficulties, the experience was incredibly fun, and it opened the door for us to meet some truly wonderful people.

During the Easter holidays, Mick and I found ourselves deep in conversation about our next travel destination. I turned to him and said, "I've taken you to my country, so now you have to take me to yours." From that moment, we began planning our six weeks holiday to the UK and Europe. This was incredibly exciting for me, as I had never been to Europe before.

The following weeks were very stressful as the research and meticulous planning began. After weeks of preparation, we realised that six weeks wouldn't suffice to see everything we wanted. Thus, we extended our journey to three months and decided to buy a motorhome upon our arrival in the UK, which would become our home for the trip. With each passing day, our anticipation and excitement grew as our adventure of a lifetime took shape.

We arranged Luke's distance education, and Teresa took on some work from school.

We felt incredibly fortunate to be able to afford this holiday. By wisely investing the money from the sale of our house in shares, we earned enough money to make our dream holiday come true.

As we were deep in the excitement of packing and planning for our dream holiday, my in-laws announced they were coming for a visit. One day, while Mick was chatting with his mum, he casually remarked, "I don't know where the kids are today." Without missing a beat, my second mum replied, "They're at their piano lessons." I cherished her deeply; she had the gift of knowing everything about everyone. Our bond was so strong that whenever I needed advice, I would call her—she was my counsellor and support person. After a long twelve months apart, it was wonderful to see them again. I truly was blessed to have the best mother-in-law.

By the middle of August, we had packed everything into the container, ready for storage. While staying at the hotel for a few days, I received an unexpected call from the airline. They offered us business class seats from Japan to London, if we flew a day later. Thrilled, I immediately asked Mick for his thoughts. He said he would think about it, but I quickly replied, "There's nothing to think about. I'm saying yes." It felt like winning the lottery.

After saying emotional goodbyes to our friends, whom we had known for only a short time, we listened to their advice on how to stay safe while travelling with kids and a baby. Their cautionary tales of babies being stolen and bags being snatched off shoulders filled me with fear. I couldn't help but wonder if we should be taking our children to places like these. Overwhelmed with worry, I surrendered my fears to Jesus and prayed for our safety.

Our journey included a stopover in Japan, providing just enough time for dinner, a shower, and a brief rest. The next day, our longest voyage began. I was quite anxious about Xavier, worrying he might not settle and would disturb other passengers. To my relief, he was exceptionally well-behaved, eating and sleeping peacefully, making our flight thoroughly enjoyable thanks to the business class seats.

After a 13-hour flight, we finally touched down in London, my heart brimming with excitement. Navigating from Heathrow Airport to Greenwich proved to be a challenging journey, especially with suitcases and a baby stroller to manage. Despite the complexities of using public transport, we persevered and successfully made it to our destination. We stayed in a charming bed and breakfast in Greenwich for a week. Each day, we caught the bus or the train to explore the heart of London. The friendly locals on the buses would often strike up conversations with us and the kids, eager to learn about life in Australia. Our days were filled with adventure and discovery as we explored the city's enchanting surroundings. Every location we visited left us in awe.

From London, we flew to Germany to purchase a motorhome, which became our home on wheels for the next six months. After picking it up, we began an incredible journey, driving back through Belgium, France, and eventually returning to England. Once back, we set out to explore the rest of the country and reconnect with family. Meeting so many relatives for the first time was thrilling, and the kids had a blast catching up with their cousins, making memories they'd treasure.

Our travels took us far and wide. We ventured up to Scotland, then across to Ireland, where we visited Mick's relatives. It was heartwarming to finally meet everyone and spend time together. From there, we explored the beauty of Wales before looping back to England.

Our next adventure took us beyond the British Isles. We crossed into France, then continued to Switzerland, back through France, and down to Italy and Spain. For an extra thrill, we even took a day trip to Africa! Each stop brought new landscapes, cultures, and experiences, turning our journey into an unforgettable family adventure.

Celebrating my 40th birthday in Olhão, Portugal was unforgettable. After a delightful dinner with my kids, Mick and I found ourselves at a bar, surrounded by a lively group of English people, while the kids went back to the van. They welcomed us at their table, and soon enough, they were buying me drinks. We sang songs, shared stories, and laughed until our sides hurt. Their warmth and kindness made the night feel magical.

19th of January 2007, was supposed to be a day of exploration and learning. We had planned to visit the naval museum; a place Mick had been eager to see for months. However, our day took a drastic turn when Mick checked his email in the morning. It was from Kerrie, his sister, said to call home urgently. With trembling hands, Mick called Kerrie to find out the news.

There was distressing news about Helen, my dear friend. She had been in a severe car accident and had to be airlifted to the Royal Alfred Hospital in Melbourne. She had suffered a brain clot and had undergone a six-hour operation. Following the surgery, the doctors placed her in an induced coma, where she would remain for the next three days. My first thought was, Helen can't die now. We haven't danced enough.

I was devastated. Overwhelmed by worry and sadness, I couldn't help but think of all the moments Helen and I had shared. The news was heartbreaking. The doctors feared that Helen might suffer permanent brain damage and could lose her ability to recognise anyone.

As the weight of this news settled in, my heart shattered. Feeling helpless and desperate to do something, anything, to help her recovery, we turned to prayer. Together, we prayed every night for Helen's healing and strength, hoping that our collective faith and love might reach her in her darkest hour.

We gathered our things and headed to town, eager to explore the marina area and visit the Monument to the Discoveries, a tribute to Portugal's illustrious explorers. At the monument, we watched an enlightening film about Lisbon's rich and varied history, highlighting its eras as a Christian, Roman, and Islamic centre. Immersing ourselves in a fascinating exhibition, we allowed the captivating displays to distract us from the morning's distressing news.

Every night before going to sleep, Mick led us in prayer for Helen's recovery. It was a blessing that we were heading back to Spain, and then to France, where we could visit Lourdes, the holy place, and pray for Helen which gave me some comfort.

The next day was Mick's birthday. Mick and I didn't know what to do but had to make a hard decision to keep going with our holiday plan. Teresa and Luke were sad with us. We had a cake for Mick and sang happy birthday after dinner. I just wanted to go and be with Helen.

The next day, we began our journey back to Spain. We had been away from home for five months and were eager to return. After a seven-hour drive, with only a brief stop for lunch, we finally arrived in Madrid. By the time we reached the caravan park, it was dark. When Mick went to hand over his passport, he realised he had left it at the caravan park in Lisbon. This caused us great concern as we considered how to retrieve it. The following day, when we tried to call the caravan park, the line was busy. Mick kept trying all day, and when they finally answered, they told us to call back the next day since the lady who had served us was not available.

In the meantime, we called Kerrie in Melbourne to check on Helen's condition. Helen had a good night, and her family had brought in her belongings to make her feel more comfortable. It was a waiting game, as she was still in a coma. We were all deeply saddened and could only pray, hoping our prayers would be answered. Next time we rang to check on Helen's condition, doctors were considering turning off the ventilator as her brain was severely damaged. She would not be able to remember anything or recognise anyone. Staying in touch with home was challenging since we didn't have internet access at our location, we had to keep driving and connect to unsecured Wi-Fi.

Despite our worries, we continued with our plans. Over the next two days, we explored Madrid, visiting the museum and the Royal Palace. The palace was stunningly decorated, an absolute marvel to behold. The weather had turned very cold, dropping to about two degrees.

Mick persisted in calling the caravan park in Lisbon about his passport. Finally, the lady offered to mail it to us in Madrid. We then drove to Toledo to spend a day exploring the town. Known for its swords and knives, Toledo was unique, set on a hill above the plains of Castilla. The medieval monuments of Arab, Jewish, and Christian heritage in the old city were breathtaking. Although it was a cold and rainy day, we made the most of our time, as we only had the day to explore.

After three days of waiting in Madrid for Mick's passport, we moved on. Our journey took us through the Pyrenees to San Sebastian, where it was snowing. We all got out to experience the snow, and the kids had a snowball fight, which was fun to watch. But it was freezing, so they quickly jumped back into the van. Even Xavier enjoyed the snow. As it was getting dark, we found a place to park for free in Biarritz in France after driving for over six hours and thankfully, there was electricity so we could plug in our heater.

We woke up early that day; Mick had set the alarm as we were driving to Lourdes. I sat and prayed the whole time Mick was driving. "Helen, you can't die yet—we haven't danced enough. You have to get better," I whispered, my voice cracking. I was so desperate I was begging Jesus and Mother Mary to give life to my dear friend again. It was the 11th day since the accident.

The drive to Lourdes was two and a half hours, but we stopped for an hour at an unsecured place to call home and the British consulate in France about Mick's passport. Mick was told that it wasn't a surprise to them; it happens a lot in Portugal. When we arrived in Lourdes, after finding the internet, Mick called the caravan park in Madrid. Thankfully, Mick's passport had arrived. We were overjoyed, a glimmer of hope amidst the darkness. They promised to post it to our next destination.

We arrived in Lourdes and went directly to the grotto where the Virgin Mary appeared 18 times to St Bernadette.

Everyone lit a candle, and we gathered in prayer. My heart was heavy as I begged Mother Mary, "Please, let Helen remember me when I visit her as soon as I get home." We had been receiving messages that Helen might not recognise anyone, and the thought was unbearable. I prayed for all my family and friends for their well-being.

We bought rosary beads and dipped them in holy water, one for each of us and for friends and one for Helen. It was a deeply spiritual experience; unlike anything I had ever felt before. I felt peace in my heart and surrendered to the higher powers and continued with the journey.

The next day, we drove to Bordeaux, a drive that took about three hours. I was both excited and surprised to see snow on people's rooftops—a sight I had never experienced before. We had to stay here while waiting for Mick's passport to arrive, which gave Mick time to fix a couple of things in the van since we planned to sell it once we reached England. This also allowed Teresa to practice the French she had been learning in school as she accompanied Mick to search for parts.

I absolutely loved Bordeaux. The atmosphere was incredibly relaxing, and I relished the chance to go out for delicious meals without having to cook. Mick called Helen's son to check on her condition, and we were relieved to hear some good news: Helen was out of intensive care, stable, but not yet fully awake. This was the news we had been anxiously waiting for.

With hope and prayers in our hearts, on the following day, February 2nd, we sent holy water and rosary beads to Kerrie in Melbourne, from Gradignan, a small town just outside Bordeaux. These were meant for Helen, and we asked Kerrie to bring them to the hospital, sprinkle the holy water on Helen, and say a prayer. That day was significant, as it also marked the birthday of Helen's daughter, who was our beloved goddaughter.

During our stay, we explored a few nearby places, each more interesting than the last. Finally, on the sixth day, Mick's passport arrived. We were overjoyed; it meant we could begin our drive toward Calais and make our way back to England.

We sold our motorhome in England, getting the asking price after a bit of a wait, which was a relief. We stopped in Japan for a quick four-day holiday and arrived home after six and half months away in March. Once everything settled, I booked a flight to Melbourne for Xavier and I to visit Helen at the end of March.

I couldn't shake the anxiety that troubled me the entire time sitting in the plane. My thoughts kept drifting to

Helen's condition and the rest of my family. I had to keep reminding myself not to talk about my own pain to my family, especially my mum. I knew I needed to focus on what truly mattered, seeing my dear friend Helen recover. My pain wasn't important; I would be fine. All I wanted was to see her get better. The only thing I knew was that she had been moved from the hospital to a rehabilitation centre, and I was desperate to be by her side.

I stayed at my in-law's place. The next day Kerrie and I visited Helen. My heart was jumping out of my body and I didn't know what to expect when I saw Helen. As soon as Kerrie and I walked into the room where Helen was sitting in a wheelchair, she saw me and started wheeling herself towards me and called my name out loud and then Kerrie's name. I quickly thanked Mother Mary for answering my prayers. I was so excited to see her talking and her remembering me. From that day on, I knew she would be fine. It was going to be a long road of recovery, but she could do it with her new partner next to her.

She couldn't remember the accident or any recent memories, but she vividly recalled moments from the past. She kept talking about her ex-husband and stories from their time in India. During one of our conversations, she asked me if I remembered the man who stood beside her at her daughter's baptism when her husband refused to be there. I told her it was Mick, my husband, who had stepped in when all the fathers were asked to stand up. She seemed surprised and said she couldn't recall who that person was. So, we continued reminiscing about the past, the only memories she seemed to hold on to.

The next day, Kerrie and I brought Xavier with us to visit Helen again. This time, she was in her room, and we could sprinkle holy water on her as I continued praying for her strength. Xavier, being his usual curious self, pressed the emergency button, and the nurses came running, only to find him laughing, completely unaware of the commotion he had caused.

Now that my heart had settled, seeing Helen and knowing that she was going to be alright by the grace of the almighty God, I had to dig deep to find all my strength to visit my family. My parents, uncle, and auntie gathered at Bella's house one night. The good thing was that we had so much to talk about. They were all worried and wanted to know about Helen's recovery, as well as the story about my uncle in the UK.

We talked about the places we visited and how much I enjoyed the holiday. But inside, I was suffering, my heart heavy with the weight of everything I kept hidden. The conversations felt distant, like they were happening to someone else, while my anger bubbled just beneath the surface. I was still angry, especially at my mum, for not supporting me again, for leaving me to carry everything alone. It wasn't the first time, but that only made it worse.

Every time I reached out, hoping this time might be different, I was left feeling abandoned, like my pain didn't matter. I kept reminding myself not to talk about my past.

Well, Mum and I never talked about my past ever again, and I kept my promise. I carried the weight of my suffering in silence. Life had to go on. There was no room for feeling sorry for myself.

Determined to move forward, I remembered my dream from when we were travelling. I had been contemplating whether to pursue an aged care or childcare course, and in my dream, I found myself in a school, upstairs in a classroom, with children sitting on the floor around me. That image stayed with me, and I knew it was a sign. My bigger picture was to one day work in a Catholic school, but I had no idea how I would get there yet.

With that goal in mind, I enrolled at TAFE to complete a childcare educator's course and began applying for jobs at various daycare centres, which meant I could get the course for a discounted price. I sent out countless applications, each one carrying the hope that it would be the start of my new career. But the rejections started coming in. No one responded. I thought that maybe a Queensland thing, and it felt like every unanswered application was a blow to my confidence. Still, I refused to give up. Even as the doors kept closing, I held onto that dream, trusting that somehow, I would find the path to where I was meant to be.

One day, I walked into a centre and handed my resume directly to the receptionist. She kindly suggested I try another centre just up the road. With nothing to lose, I followed her advice. The next day, to my shock and amazement, the director of that centre called me. She didn't ask for an interview. She simply offered me the job and asked if I could start the very next day.

It felt like a dream. All my efforts had finally paid off. I thanked Jesus for guiding me through what had felt like an impossible journey. For so long, I had doubted myself, wondering what I was doing wrong. But from that moment on, my life changed.

The best part about going to work was having Xavier at the same centre with me. On the first day, when I dropped him off in his room, he cried and cried, desperately reaching for me. My heart ached for him; it was the first time he had been left with strangers. Throughout the day, I kept checking on him and by morning break, he had finally calmed down, thanks to the wonderful ladies in his room who were so accommodating.

I loved my job, working two to three days a week as a relief, which meant I had to be ready every morning for a possible call. It was my first job in Townsville after not working for someone else in over ten years. Everything about it was fulfilling, working alongside wonderful staff, meeting parents, grandparents, and children. My life became so busy, balancing work and studying at the same time. I didn't have time to feel sad or dwell on the past. My days were full, and I embraced it all.

There were times when I felt so overwhelmed studying at home by myself. It had been 24 years since I last tackled assignments in high school, and the years hadn't made it any easier. The only things I had done before I met Mick were six weeks of typing, photography, and computer courses. I remember using the TV as a monitor. Simple tasks took longer than they should have, and I blamed the monster who had stolen my love for learning, the one who caused me not to finish school. Often, I got lost in angry thoughts, blaming those who didn't take care of me, who didn't support me when I needed it most.

But I never cried. Instead, I carried a sadness so deep it made my heart ache. There were days when I didn't even know why I was sad, but I kept pushing forward.

The best weeks of study were when we gathered in the classroom at TAFE for workshops. Being in a group made everything easier, the teacher, the students, all there to help when I got stuck. I loved the energy of studying with others. It felt like learning came alive again.

A couple of months later, I was back on the plane with the family to Melbourne, this time to celebrate two special occasions: Kerrie's 40th and her son's 18th birthday. I felt a burst of excitement knowing how much this celebration meant, not just for them, but for me as well. Kerrie had always been there for me through so many moments in my life, and I wanted her to feel truly special this time around.

Kerrie and I visited Helen at her home. She was doing okay, but she was struggling. She had lost her sense of smell and taste, and she couldn't read or write anymore. Most of her recent memories were gone. Her new partner and her kids were by her side, helping her get back on her feet.

Every day, I kept her in my prayers but seeing her like this made my heart ache. Helen used to cook the most amazing dosa and curries for me whenever I visited. Now, she couldn't cook, and even if she tried, she wouldn't be able to taste her own food. It felt so wrong, knowing that someone who had given me so much joy through her cooking had lost that simple pleasure.

I visited my parents with the three kids, as Mick refused to go. He was still deeply disappointed with my family for not supporting me. I had little choice. Despite everything, I loved my parents, and I wanted my children to have a relationship with Nani and Nana. My heart ached, and anxiety twisted in my stomach. Still, I was proud of myself for continuing to visit them every time I was in Melbourne, holding onto the hope that one day all my pain would disappear, and I would finally feel like I belonged in the family again.

When Teresa turned 16 in November, my mind went into overdrive, consumed by fear. All I could think about was how I was going to keep her safe. I became overprotective, constantly on edge, and the idea of her going out with boys was terrifying. I was grateful she attended an all-girls school, though we hadn't chosen it for that reason. We believed single-sex education was better for learning, but now it felt like a small layer of protection.

Teresa, of course, didn't know my full story, and because of that, we clashed constantly. Every disagreement felt like a tug-of-war between her desire for freedom and my overwhelming need to keep her safe.

In December, after three years, we finally got to spend Christmas with the family at my in-laws', my favourite celebration. It was so good to be together again, to enjoy the moment, and just be myself. There were about 30 of us, filling the house with joy and warmth. It felt comforting to be part of something so familiar.

But when I visited my parents with the three kids, nothing had changed - the same uneasy silence, the same tension. By now, I had become very good at hiding my emotions, wearing a mask of calm and composure. Inside, I was still hurt, still angry, but I had learned to bury it deep. I smiled, made small talk, and pretended it didn't bother me, but the weight of it was always there, weighing me down.

One day before school finished, Teresa came home bursting with excitement. She told us about an opportunity to sponsor a student from Italy who wanted to learn English and immerse herself in Australian culture. We thought, why not? It sounded like a wonderful experience for all of us.

A 17-year-old girl named Guila arrived shortly after Australia day in 2008. She stayed with us for six months, attending school with Teresa. As a family, we made sure she got the full Australian experience. Teresa and Guila even travelled down to Melbourne to visit the family. Once a week, Guila cooked us authentic Italian dishes for dinner, and every so often, she would treat us to a homemade dessert, which was yummy.

When Guila first arrived, she could only speak a little bit of English, managing a few words here and there. But by the time she left, she was forming sentences, her confidence in the language growing with each day. It was amazing to witness how much she blossomed during her time with us.

Luke and I travelled to Sydney for my cousin's wedding for a long weekend.

The wedding was beautiful, and it held a deep meaning for me. This cousin was born just nine days after I left Fiji, and I never got the chance to truly connect with her. I had taken care of her two older sisters, but with her, there was always a gap. Watching her walk down the aisle filled me with both joy and pride, knowing how much she had grown. She combined Indian and Australian culture in her wedding, as she was marrying an Australian man, and it was so beautiful to witness the blending of traditions. It reflected her identity perfectly. We danced, ate, and reconnected with a cousin who was a huge part of my life growing up after over 20 years and her son who travelled from Canada. I felt the joy in my heart just being in the moment with the extended family, cherishing every moment of that special day.

The best part of that weekend, though, was seeing my mum again. My emotions ran high, and all I wanted was to give her a hug strong enough to take my pain away. I was always searching for healing, wishing that the weight of my emotions would somehow miraculously vanish, but the hurt lingered, leaving me aching for that permanent relief.

Teresa went to Sydney for World Youth Day with her school, which was very exciting for her, but I was worried and prayed for her safety. She and her friends had an amazing time together and came home with their hearts filled with joy. Teresa was always eager to participate in everything at school. I was always involved in all her activities.

She never got into trouble, so when I received a phone call saying Teresa was suspended for putting some colour in the fountain on the Strand as a joke at the end of Year 12, I couldn't believe it. Mick had to face the principal, and he wasn't happy about it.

Regardless, I felt so proud of her when she asked me to wear my dress that I had worn for an Indian wedding, for her graduation. Teresa, who had admired it for years as it hung in the cupboard, dreamt of wearing it for her graduation. Fifteen years later, that dress found a new purpose. Her request filled me with immense happiness, knowing that the dress, once a symbol of my struggles, now represented her achievement and joy. When she stepped out wearing it, she looked like a princess, radiating confidence and grace. Mick and I were filled with pride as her parents, watching her take this significant step toward her future.

For schoolies week, Mick and I didn't want Teresa to go to Airlie Beach with her friends. The idea of so many 17 and 18-year-olds drinking alcohol for the first time just terrified me. Somehow, Teresa persisted, and we had to agree on one condition. I had to drive her there, three and a half hours, just to see for myself before dropping her off.

Once I saw the setup, I felt better knowing there were volunteers at the events to help if the kids got into trouble. Still, I prayed for her safety and that of her friends. My heart swelled with pride when Teresa told me later how she took care of her drunk friends, looking after them when they couldn't manage on their own. That's my girl, I thought.

Luke graduated from primary school the same year, and I was swept up in a whirlwind of emotions as life seemed to move so quickly. Christmas that year was especially exciting because my in-laws joined us, making it feel more like a true family celebration. We hired a van and took a holiday to Cairns and the surrounding areas for a week. It was a blast, especially getting to spend time with my second mum, something that made the trip even more meaningful.

Xavier started kindergarten three days a week, while Luke embarked on his high school journey, and Teresa began her first year at university and started working at age care. Mick had just started a new job after finding out drafting wasn't for him, and I had recently completed my Certificate III and moved on to studying for a Diploma in Children's Services. Life was very busy. With Teresa now licensed to drive, she took on the responsibility of picking up her brothers on the days I had to work long hours. Having my permanent hours in place brought a sense of stability, making it easier to manage the household.

Mick started coaching football skills to Luke when it became clear just how naturally gifted he was. Watching him play with other teams, it was evident that Luke had a unique flair, pulling off fancy tricks and moves that left everyone in awe, especially his mum and dad. On the field, he was mesmerising. But rather than celebrate his creativity and skill, the coaches told him to stop showing off and just pass the ball. This frustrated Luke and us deeply. We could see how much he loved the game, and nothing was going to make him give it up, not when his dream was to become a football player.

With all the stress surrounding football, it was a welcome distraction to take a family trip to Sydney for my cousin's 21st birthday and her dad's 40th combined surprise party. The excitement of it all lifted our spirits. When the moment came, both father and daughter were completely surprised. The party was so much fun, we danced the night away, savouring the time spent with family.

My mum, auntie, and uncle had travelled from Melbourne, and it was a relief to see my mum again. As always, I hoped she would finally talk to me about my pain, to acknowledge it but just like last time, she acted as if nothing had happened. It hurt, but I tried to focus on the joy of the moment, enjoying the company of family while quietly carrying that burden in my heart.

For Teresa's 18th birthday, we threw a party in a hall filled with music, food, and plenty of alcohol for the 18-year-olds. It was a lively celebration, and once again, my in-laws,

Kerrie, and two of Teresa's cousins made the trip up from Melbourne. My auntie, uncle, cousin, her husband and two-year-old baby flew from Sydney. Having the family around brought a warmth and joy to the event. It was a memorable night. Teresa met her first boyfriend after she turned 18 and she called me at work to give me the good news. I didn't freak out, I just accepted it. I surprised myself.

We bought our first property in Queensland on the 22nd of December 2009 in Hermit Park, a high-set house with a beautiful backyard for Xavier to play in and a downstairs space for Teresa to have her own area. Our first Christmas in the new house was exciting. The five of us sat together at the table, surrounded by plenty of food and cheer, feeling proud of our small achievement.

Things intensified between Teresa and me after she turned 18. She would go out with friends, staying out late, and I wouldn't sleep until I heard the car door shut, signalling she was home. The stress of worrying about her became unbearable, and my inner suffering grew heavier, still weighed down by anger toward my mum.

Xavier got accepted into St Joseph's School, just five minutes up the road, a place that already felt like home. We had attended the parish a year ago, and when Xavier began school, I was welcomed with such warmth that it instantly put me at ease. I liked the feel of the school, the sense of community, and the kindness of the staff, especially Xavier's prep teacher, who seemed genuinely caring.

I continued working at the daycare centre, sometimes staying until 6 p.m. to close up, then hurrying home to tend to the family. Life felt busy, but manageable, until things between Teresa and us escalated again. The tension had been growing, and it all came to a head when the police were called after her friend accused us of mistreating her. Teresa left home, choosing to stay with her friend, and my heart broke. I missed her more than I could express, and although we stayed in touch through texts, the house felt emptier without her.

After three long months, Teresa asked if she could come back home. I welcomed her with open arms, just happy to have my daughter back under our roof. Soon after, Teresa met her new boyfriend, and for a while, things seemed to go well. We were genuinely happy for her.

But when she found out that Mick and I didn't approve of her boyfriend staying over, especially not sleeping downstairs, it created new friction. Mick was very strict about this, and no matter how much I wished I could change his mind, I couldn't. The situation became tense again, and Teresa started spending most nights at his place instead. I felt torn. Part of me wished we didn't have this rule, but Mick's stance was firm. Things took a turn when she refused to come with us to the Gold Coast for a family holiday. Her absence left me heartbroken. I felt like I was losing control, and I didn't know how to fix things between us. The confusion and sadness weighed heavily on me again.

Despite the emotional strain, I had to pull myself together. My auntie and her family had driven up from Sydney to join us on the Gold Coast, and I didn't want to dampen the experience for the rest of the family. It was our first time on the Gold Coast, and the kids were buzzing with excitement. We visited the theme parks, and all four kids had an amazing time. It was wonderful to see my boys connecting with their cousins. For a week, I put my pain aside and embraced the moment. We all had a wonderful time together, and despite everything, I cherished those memories.

Soon after, Mick changed his job again. This time, he was given a company vehicle and was constantly on the road, travelling from job to job. In the little spare time he had, he came up with the idea of building a cold room to hire out for some extra income. It was typical of him to think of new ways to keep us moving forward.

We started supporting the local football team, Fury. Our love for football ran deep, and we didn't miss a single home game. It became a tradition for us, something we looked forward to watching together. So, when Teresa, her friend, and Xavier returned from Melbourne on Xavier's

6th birthday, we celebrated by going to the game. The atmosphere was electric, and it felt like the perfect way to end the day.

But when we came back home, the mood shifted instantly. The front door was wide open. When we walked in, every drawer was open. Someone had broken into our house and stolen my expensive jewellery, along with all our passports. We were devastated. It wasn't just the loss of the valuables, it was the feeling of violation, knowing that a stranger had been inside our home. Xavier was especially affected. He was so scared that night, refusing to sleep in his room while Luke was still in Melbourne.

The very next day, determined to restore some sense of security, we went to the pound and bought a dog. Teresa named her Ruby. From that moment on, Ruby became a part of our family, bringing us a bit of comfort and joy after the shock of that terrifying day.

Just as that frustration was weighing heavily on me, we began preparing for the cyclone that was set to hit Townsville on the 2nd of February 2011. It was my first time experiencing a cyclone, and I was terrified for my kids. I couldn't stop thinking about whether our 60-year-old house would still be standing once the storm passed.

We prepared as best we could, barricading ourselves in the safest, smallest part of the house, the hallway, where we pushed our heavy dining table up against two walls for added protection. As the wind howled and grew stronger, the fear settled deep inside me. My mind raced, imagining the worst possible outcome. I just wanted my children to be safe and the house to be standing. I prayed constantly for our protection.

During the night, we heard the loud, crushing sound of our beautiful backyard tree falling. My heart sank, but as morning broke, we saw that the tree had only destroyed part of the fence, narrowly missing the house. We were all so grateful that our home remained intact, and above all, that we still had a roof over our heads.

I flew to Melbourne for a work reunion with some of the most important people in my life—Kerrie, Helen, and my sister Kelly, who joined us in the later years. I worked at Stegbar for nine and a half years, a place that holds a special spot in my heart. It was there that my life changed for the better. The friendships I formed during that time have stood the test of time, and every time I visit Melbourne, without fail, we come together.

These people have become more than just friends; they are like family to me. There's no judgment, only warmth and understanding, and it always feels so good to reconnect with them. My heart swells with joy every time I see their familiar faces, and I'm reminded of how fortunate I am to have them in my life. Stegbar wasn't just a job—it was the beginning of lifelong bonds that continue to uplift and enrich my life today.

Luke constantly had to defend his approach on the field and even at school. He could juggle the ball over 2,000 times without letting it drop. Mick would train Luke for most mornings before school. Despite his dedication and talent, Luke's style wasn't appreciated by everyone. Some coaches and even his teammates seemed to resent the way he played, and it led to countless headaches for our family.

The worst incident came during high school. While the boys were playing, a classmate deliberately poured urine from a bottle all over Luke's school bag, which had been left outside with the others. What made it even worse was that a bystander, his classmate, who witnessed it, did nothing to stop it.

When the teacher called to tell me, I was utterly speechless. How could something so cruel happen to my Luke? Mick and I were devastated. We didn't know how to comfort him, and it hurt even more that Mick was away for work. The next morning, the bystander's parents showed up at our house. I didn't expect them, but when the mother and I saw each other, we just hugged and cried. Their son had written a letter of apology to Luke, and they insisted he read it out to him in person. The parents apologised on his behalf, but we were all in shock.

Later that day, Luke came to me and said, "Mum, I just want to go to Melbourne to be with the family." My heart broke as I realised how much he needed to get away. I booked him a flight, and he went to spend Christmas at granny and grandad's house with the family down there. I cried for days afterward, haunted by the fact that someone could hurt my child so deeply and I couldn't protect him. I felt helpless to shield him from the cruelty of the world.

Luke was always excited to fly solo to Melbourne for his football workshops. His grandad and granny would be waiting for him at the airport, ready to drive him to the sessions. I was so grateful for their support, knowing they were always there to help him pursue his passion.

With so much happening at home and work, I wasn't coping. The stress was piling up, and all I could think about was running away to a deserted island where no one could find me. I spent weeks contemplating how to escape the chaos, but deep down, I knew I couldn't just leave everything behind. Still, something had to change.

One evening, as I scrolled through the newsletter, a glimmer of hope appeared. A Tuckshop convenor position was advertised at Xavier's school. It was something different, something manageable. Maybe this was the change I needed. Lucky for me, the timing felt right.

The very next morning, I called the office and spoke to the principal. He gave me a date for an interview. When the day arrived, I came home early from work to get changed and prepare myself. As I was sitting and relaxing, the phone rang. It was the principal asking if I was still coming to the interview because it was scheduled for 10 minutes ago.

I froze. My heart sank, and my first thought was, "Don't bother going; I'm not going to get this job." Still, I forced myself up and headed to the school.

When I walked into the interview room, three people were already seated: the principal, the assistant principal, and a mum from the Parents and Friends committee. My heart pounded, my stomach tied in knots with nerves, and I felt completely out of place. This was my first ever interview. Their eyes were on me, and I struggled to steady my breath, but I pushed through, answering their questions as best as I could. Somehow, despite the nerves and the self-doubt, I got the job. I think Jesus was with me that day.

At last, I was going to work in a school, somewhere I had loved being as a young girl. The excitement of seeing my dream come true filled me with joy. But it was bittersweet as I said goodbye to the staff, parents, and children at the Daycare centre where I'd spent so many memorable days. It warmed my heart, though, that they invited me back to work there during school holidays.

My new role at the school gave me the perfect balance. I was able to help in Xavier's class while working five hours a day, which meant I could still manage the drop-offs, pick-ups, and taking the boys to their activities. It felt like the best of both worlds, being involved in the kids' school life without sacrificing my time with them.

The staff were incredibly welcoming, and despite the initial chaos, I quickly began to feel at home. Within days, I found myself looking forward to my shifts and feeling a sense of belonging in this little corner of the school community.

I met some wonderful mothers and grandmothers who came to volunteer, helping prepare and serve the children during morning tea and lunch. Their kindness and commitment were inspiring. At the end of every year, I organised a thank you dinner for all the volunteers. It became a tradition I loved, filled with joy, good food, and appreciation and a place of healing.

I started working every Saturday for six hours at the aged care facility where Teresa worked. It was a new experience, stepping into a different role, but I enjoyed being there, helping the elderly serve dinner. I felt sad thinking about my mum and why I was so angry with her. During school holidays, I took on extra hours, working three days a week at the daycare. The arrangement worked well for a while, allowing me to balance work and home life. I could be there for my family when they needed me and still contribute financially as I didn't want my boys to miss out on activities as Mick's wages were paying the bills.

But eventually, something had to give. Juggling everything took its toll. With work, home responsibilities, and my studies, I realised I couldn't keep going at that pace. I made the difficult decision to pause my diploma studies, even though I was only halfway through the program. It wasn't easy, but I knew it was the only way to manage everything without burning out.

Luke celebrated his 16th birthday at home with a few of his friends from school. The house buzzed with playful energy as the kids gathered around, teasing and cheering him on while he opened his gifts. It was heartwarming to see Luke so happy, just being himself, enjoying the moment. His smile, so carefree, was the kind of thing that made all the hard days feel worth it.

As a mother, I've always tried my best to give my children everything they needed to be happy, to create moments like these where they could feel safe and loved. But sometimes, no matter how hard you try, life has its way of throwing challenges at them and at us. And there's nothing you can do but be there, to stand by their side, offering comfort when words fall short and strength when the world feels heavy.

I was overjoyed when Helen invited the whole family to her wedding in October 2012. Unfortunately, we couldn't all go because of work and school commitments, so Teresa and I made the trip together. Teresa and I were getting along well, especially since she had settled into a secure apartment with her boyfriend. It was a peaceful moment between us.

When Helen appeared in her stunning red dress, it felt as though time stood still. The moment she walked up the aisle, her smile radiated warmth and strength, a reflection of all she had endured. Tears welled up in my eyes as I watched her, my heart swelling with gratitude. I had prayed for this day, for her recovery, and for the chance to witness such joy in her life again. Silently, I thanked Mother Mary and Jesus for their blessings, for guiding Helen through her hardships and bringing us to this moment of celebration.

My heart was so full that I couldn't resist the pull of the music. When a lively song began, Kerrie and I found ourselves alone on the dance floor. The two of us danced, just letting go, not caring that everyone was watching. It was pure joy to see my dear friend found true love again, and for that moment, everything felt perfect.

It was also perfect timing to celebrate another milestone, a niece's 18th birthday. I've always felt a special bond with her, having picked her and her brother up from school in their younger years, spending afternoons together as I helped her with homework. Watching her grow into the person she is today, now teaching at a high school, makes Mick and me incredibly proud. She's living her dreams, and knowing we played a small part in her journey warms my heart.

A couple of weeks later, we celebrated Teresa's 21st birthday, and once again, my tribe from Melbourne arrived, Granny, Grandad, Kerrie, and two cousins. Teresa didn't want a big party; instead, she asked for money as her present, hoping to use it for a trip to the UK and Europe with her two friends.

We went out for a lovely dinner with some of her friends and family. It was such a beautiful night, being all together again, sharing time together and making memories. Two weeks later, Teresa and her two friends were on a plane, ready to embark on the adventure of their lives. I was so proud of my daughter, not just for her achievements but for her confidence and independence.

As I watched her leave, I prayed for the girl's safety and their journey ahead. They had an amazing time, travelling for seven weeks, exploring new places and experiences. It seemed life was unfolding beautifully. The whole family gathered in Melbourne for a momentous occasion: the first wedding of a grandchild, Kerrie's only son. The bride looked stunning, and the entire wedding party radiated elegance and joy.

One day in May, while I was working in the Tuckshop during lunch, I noticed Xavier playing basketball with his friend. Suddenly, he fell and screamed out in pain. My heart dropped. Without thinking, I ran outside to help. When I reached him, he was writhing on the ground, crying in agony. His face was pale, and I could tell something was terribly wrong.

The teacher and principal rushed over, and after taking one look at Xavier, they immediately called for an ambulance. His arm was broken, and badly. His screams echoed across the court, and as he passed out from the pain, my heart clenched. I was helpless, standing there, unable to ease his suffering. When the ambulance arrived, he was given the whistle for relief. I went with him. It was our first time riding in one, but all I could think about was his pain and how scared he must have been.

After what felt like endless hours of waiting at the hospital, the x-ray results came back, a compound fracture. The sight of the bone piercing through his skin made my stomach churn. It was worse than I imagined. I felt sick, and there was nothing I could do to take away the pain. All I could do was pray.

The hospital staff were amazing, and what gave me a bit of comfort was seeing Mick. He has been working at the hospital for the last two years and came over to support us. His familiar face brought a sense of calm in the middle of this nightmare.

Xavier had to undergo surgery to have a rod placed in his arm to realign the bones, followed by a cast. It was heartbreaking to see him in so much pain. The next day, Teresa came over to stay with him so I could go to work, as she was now living with a couple of her friends, renting an apartment. The following months were tough, no swimming, no piano lessons, and no football, just three long months of recovery, watching him struggle. Then, he had to face another surgery to remove the rod.

Those were difficult days for both of us, but especially for Xavier. Seeing my baby endure so much pain shattered me in ways I can't even describe. Yet all I could do was stand by him and pray that he would heal fully.

In June, my cousin Jane and her two kids came over for a visit, a reunion I had been waiting for after not seeing her for 12 years. It felt like reconnecting with an old friend, the kind you fall back into step with as if no time had passed. We went to Magnetic Island, where we had the best time together. Luke had already built a bond with them, as he had stayed at their place in Brisbane for football trips through school.

I've always loved Jane. We first grew close when I moved to Australia, sharing so many memories and milestones. But after our weddings, we somehow lost touch. Seeing her again made me realise how much I'd missed that connection. It was as if we were picking up where we left off, and the warmth of our bond returned effortlessly.

One Saturday morning in November, while Xavier was simply walking across the footpath at home, he tripped and fell. In an instant, he broke the same arm again. We couldn't believe it was happening. It felt surreal, like a nightmare repeating itself. This time, though, he wasn't screaming like the last; there was a quiet, almost eerie calm about him.

We quickly called an ambulance, and I went with him to the hospital, my heart weighed down with worry. After the examination, the doctor confirmed it was just a fracture, thankfully it wasn't a compound fracture. Nevertheless a surgery was needed to put pins in to hold together the bones for alignment and healing. He would have to wear a cast for the next three months. It was a relief, but also a challenge, knowing how long he'd have to cope with it. All I wanted was to wrap him in cotton wool and keep him close to me.

While Xavier was recovering, Luke's high school graduation was approaching, and it was an emotional time for all of us. Mick and I had to write him a letter, something heartfelt that he could open at school. It was part of a surprise organised for the boys, and sitting down to write those letters brought so many memories flooding back. I was overwhelmed with emotion, thinking about Luke finishing school and his dreams of pursuing football overseas.

During the ceremony, Luke looked so handsome in his suit, and as we sat there watching him, I felt such an immense sense of pride. I couldn't believe how quickly time had passed, but seeing him standing there, ready to step into the world, made all the challenges and late nights worth it. We were all so proud of his achievement, and I couldn't help but feel excited about what was to come.

This final Christmas was filled with a mix of excitement and sadness, as my two children were preparing to move overseas. Teresa had made plans to move to the UK, while Luke was gearing up for his journey to Spain to chase his football dream. Meanwhile, my biggest concern was Xavier having a surgery on his arm again to get the pins out, as the doctor didn't want him to travel with it on. Thankfully, he got it off just in time, a few days before we flew out.

My in-laws arrived a week before our trip to take care of the house, dog, and business.

We stopped in Dubai for three nights, carving out some special family fun time. Everything about the city was grand, and we absolutely loved it. But what made it truly magical was that we were experiencing it all together, as a family. Each moment felt like a gift, as we embraced the excitement of new opportunities and the simple joy of making memories, we knew would last a lifetime. It was more than just the city, it was us, sharing in the adventure, growing closer with every experience.

Next stop was Milan, Italy, for two nights. We missed this city the last time we were in Italy, so it felt like a perfect opportunity to experience it now. We caught the train to Milan airport, and this was the day I had been dreading. As we navigated through the bustling terminal, the weight of what was about to happen settled heavily in my chest. My heart ached as we said goodbye to Teresa. She walked toward a different gate, her path leading to the UK while ours took us to Seville, Spain, for a week. I kept hoping she would change her mind, that she would turn around and come running back to join us. But she didn't. She was gone, disappearing into the crowd.

Something shifted in my soul that day, a deep sadness took root. It wasn't just the distance between us; it was the feeling of her stepping into a new chapter, one I wasn't part of. The silence that followed her departure was more than just physical. It was the quiet echo of a door closing. I couldn't shake the sense that something had been lost, and I didn't know how to get it back. As I sat on the plane, a question rose in my mind: Did my mum and second mum feel this same pain when we left Melbourne to settle in Townsville?

My mum must have been angry and hurt when we left Melbourne, not knowing how to support me. Her anger became hurtful words that have lingered in my heart for so long, words that I've carried with me like a burden. I never knew how to let them go, never knew how to forgive her. It was a wound that never quite healed, only festered with time. Sitting there, miles away from the past, I wondered if I had ever fully understood her pain, or if I was still tangled on my own, unsure of how to bridge the gap between us as I stepped into my own new chapter.

After spending a week in the beautiful city of Seville, we flew to Valencia to help settle Luke. It took us three long weeks to find him a football team and secure a room in an older lady's house. My heart ached, and I wasn't sure if I'd be able to leave him behind in Spain. It felt like history was repeating itself, reminding me of the day I left Fiji at 17, not knowing the language or what awaited me. Now Luke was in the same position, alone in a foreign country, with only his dreams to keep him company.

To help him adjust, we enrolled him in a week of intensive Spanish classes, where the teacher spoke not a word of English in the classroom. Watching him struggle to grasp the language, my heart broke for him. Every misstep brought back memories of my own difficult beginnings.

I wanted to protect him, shield him from the challenges, but I knew this was his journey to take.

In the meantime, we immersed ourselves in the vibrant life of Valencia. We watched a couple of football games, the atmosphere crackling with excitement and energy, making Luke's dream feel within reach. The city was alive with the Fallas festival, where fireworks exploded even during the day, keeping us on our toes. We marvelled at the enormous statues each group had meticulously decorated for weeks. This festival was celebrated for spring and paid tribute to St Joseph, the patron saint of carpenters. But the most breathtaking moment came on the last night of the festival when, one by one, these beautiful creations were set ablaze and burned to the ground, their bright flames lighting up the sky. It was a bittersweet reminder of how quickly things could change, just like how I would soon leave Luke in this new world to follow his own path.

Before we left, I taught him how to cook butter chicken and spaghetti bolognese so he could at least eat healthy meals. Luke was incredible. He faced everything with determination and grace. Mick did his best as a father, supporting Luke's dream in every way he could. But deep down, all I wanted was to go home with all my children by my side. I had to be brave, and I prayed to Jesus to give me strength.

We visited Teresa for a week. I needed to see with my own eyes where she was living and working, to give my heart some peace. She was working in a pub, living upstairs, guided by an Australian girl she met at the backpackers. She had settled in the beautiful countryside of Kent. The quiet charm of the place was comforting, but what truly amazed me was how quickly she had adapted to her new life. Teresa had already learned how to navigate her way to London by train. My heart swelled with admiration for her courage, for being so brave and independent in a foreign country.

On the way back from the UK, we stopped at Jane's house for a couple of days. It was a warm visit, and we saw Mama and Mami, my mum's eldest brother and his wife, Mama, whom I hadn't seen in a long time. The reunion was bittersweet, filled with memories and catching up on years that had quietly slipped by. This Mama was there all those years ago when Mick went to confront the predator. However, this same Mama didn't come to my wedding, a hurt I had to forgive to find peace within myself. But I also remembered that it was this Mama who, along with Mami, drove two hours to help Kelly and her kids escape domestic violence, giving us both a better future.

When we returned home, it was so good to see my in-laws there. Nothing was hard for them; they did an amazing job taking care of everything. But as soon as they left, Mick and I struggled. We had to move forward, but without our two children, it felt incomplete. Their absence weighed heavily on me, and I worried about them. My heart ached every single day. The longing and missing consumed me, casting a shadow over everything. I couldn't shake the sadness that had settled deep within me.

Thank God I had Xavier to care for; it was during this time I realised why he took so long to choose us as parents. His presence gave me a sense of purpose, something to focus on, a distraction from the heaviness that lingered in my chest. My work, church community, and the support of friends and family kept me moving forward, one day at a time.

Teresa travelled to Spain to celebrate Luke's 18th birthday, joining him and some friends he had made from all over the world. Yet, as September rolled around, the excitement of the summer faded, and reality hit. Things weren't going as planned with football. The Spanish team had their own priorities, and Luke found himself sidelined as they focused on developing their local players first.

Despite his talent and hard work, opportunities were becoming scarce, and the dream he had held onto so tightly seemed to be slipping through his fingers. By November, the uncertainty became too much to bear. Teresa, always the caring and protective older sister, stepped in. She arranged for Luke to move to London, where she had secured a job for him at a pub and even found him accommodation. Though his path had taken an unexpected turn, knowing that Teresa had his back gave Luke the strength to face this new chapter with hope.

As Christmas approached, the sadness deepened. The festive lights and cheerful atmosphere contrasted with the emptiness I felt inside. More than anything, I wanted to be with the family in Melbourne, to escape the quiet of our home and surround myself with the love and noise of those I held close. The pull to be near them was strong, and it felt like only being with them could fill the void left by my children's absence. I kept praying to Jesus, asking Him to show me how to make this pain disappear in my heart.

On New Year's Eve, while working in the garden, something shifted inside me. As I was pulling out the weeds, a thought came to me with a clarity I hadn't felt in years. I needed to send a message of gratitude to my eldest sister in Melbourne. It had been ten years since we'd truly connected, and I wasn't even sure where to begin. But the more I thought about it, the more certain I became that this was something I had to do.

I found her on Facebook, and with trembling hands, I typed out a simple message: Thank you for bringing me to Australia. It felt so small compared to what she had done for me, but it was the most honest thing I could say. I pressed send without expecting a reply.

To my surprise, she responded almost immediately. Her words were warm and filled with love, and I felt an overwhelming sense of joy wash over me. It was as if a weight had lifted from my chest. Suddenly, I had this surge of energy, and before I knew it, I was lifting large rocks and carrying them to another part of the garden. Each step felt lighter, and I marvelled at how much strength was freed from that one act of gratitude.

The pain hadn't completely vanished, but for the first time in years, I felt a glimmer of hope. It was the beginning of something new.

For Mick's 50th birthday in January, I planned a special trip to Brisbane so we could watch the Socceroos play in a World Cup match. It felt like the perfect way to celebrate such a milestone, combining Mick's love for football with a family getaway.

After Brisbane, we flew to Melbourne to continue celebrating with the family, and we caught another game there. We stayed at my in-laws' new place, a smaller house with a small backyard. This was a bit of a shock as I had been so used to going to the old place for 27 years, Mick's childhood home, but soon we adjusted.

It was wonderful to be surrounded by loved ones, especially when my sister and I hugged each other at my auntie's house. I had missed her so much, and despite the circumstances that had kept us apart, in that moment, everything felt right. The entire trip, from football matches to family reunions.

Meanwhile, Luke was in the UK, training with a couple of football teams. Despite the opportunity, he didn't enjoy the cold UK winter and missed home. After over a year away, he travelled around Europe with two of his girlfriends from Australia, and they had a blast exploring new places together. He returned home in March; we were overjoyed to get him back.

But we felt he wasn't quite the same, and that worried me. He seemed distant, like the spark he once had had faded. To lift his spirits, Mick came up with an idea. Knowing Luke's love for cars, he suggested we buy him a sports car, something that might rekindle a spark of excitement. Luke, being as responsible as ever, insisted on paying back every dollar. He hated the thought of owing anyone money, even his parents. We went along with it, hoping this gesture would bring some joy back into his life.

I got a phone call from Dad asking me to come to his 80th birthday celebration, an Indian prayer meeting with family and friends, planned for May 2015. He said he would pay for my flight. I couldn't believe what I was hearing. I was overjoyed that my dad wanted me there, and for the first time in a long while, I really felt his love. But I hadn't been to one of these gatherings in years. I didn't know what to wear or how to act. Part of me wanted to say no, to stay away from all the emotions and memories, but Mick said I should go. He encouraged me, reminding me how much it meant to be included.

Sitting on the plane with Xavier by my side brought me some comfort. I thought maybe this was a sign, maybe my prayers had been answered, and this was the opportunity to make peace with my past. We stayed at my in-laws' place again, which was familiar, but the dread in my stomach never fully went away.

On the day of the event, as we drove to the prayer meeting, anxiety churned in my gut as I whispered a silent prayer for strength. *This is my family*, I kept telling myself. *No one here is going to hurt me.* I was wearing a black top with silver buttons but I felt strangely out of place in it.

When we arrived, I was relieved to have made it safely, but my nerves hadn't calmed. I clung to Xavier as if he were my anchor in a sea of unease. My dad came to the door to welcome us. At that moment my heart felt my father's love. Seeing my dad's friends, many of whom didn't even recognise me, brought on a wave of shame. Half of me desperately wanted to belong, to feel the joy that everyone else seemed to share. The other half of me was struggling with feelings of guilt and confusion. Why was I ashamed? I had done nothing wrong. All I could think about was how I had married a white man and changed my religion. It was a part of my life, but was it really the reason for this disconnect?

The sight of my mum, sisters, niece, auntie, and uncle, all gathered in one place, filled me with a bittersweet sense of reunion. But then, amidst the chatter and laughter, I saw him - the predator. There he was, mingling with the crowd, smiling as though nothing had ever happened. A sickening feeling rose in my stomach, thinking of all the moments I had missed, all the suffering I had gone through, while he walked free, unbothered.

I forced myself to stay calm. This wasn't the time or place to confront the past. What good would it do to cause a scene here, at Dad's celebration? What was I hoping to achieve? I kept everything under control, but inside, I was a storm.

The next day, we went out for dinner to celebrate my father-in-law's 70th birthday with the family. It was a warm gathering. I felt privileged to be part of another milestone. It was one of those moments where the importance of family was deeply felt. I could just be myself again, a little more at ease without any worries and anxiety. There was something soothing about being surrounded by loved ones, celebrating life's simple joys.

I had bought a Mother's Day card but couldn't bring myself to write anything on it. For ten years, it sat untouched in my drawer, a silent reminder of my pain. Every year, I would take it out, only to put it back again. But after a decade of carrying this burden, I decided that enough was enough. It was Mother's Day again, and this time, I brought the card with me. Handing it to my mum felt significant. This card, which had caused me so much heartache over the years, finally found its place in her hands. It mattered that I gave it to her.

My mother's health had deteriorated; she started forgetting names, places, people and events. The pain in my heart grew heavier as I witnessed her decline. She had been such a strong woman, always caring for everyone else, and now she needed looking after. I loved my mum so much. Every time I visited Melbourne; I had to see her. I wanted to tell her how much I loved her but never found the right moment. Yet every time I saw her, my heart was filled with that unspoken love.

All these years, I had felt that I caused suffering for my parents. Even though I was the victim of abuse, I somehow felt responsible for the shame. My intention was never to hurt my parents. I never wanted to disrespect them or cause them any pain. As events unfolded in my past, I began to feel like I was a shameful daughter, always causing trouble. There were times when I overheard people say, "I didn't know you had another daughter." This was hard to hear, as if I was indeed the shameful daughter my parents kept a secret about. Later when I realised that none of this was my fault, I needed to heal from this pain and find peace in my heart to forgive and understand the decisions made by my parents.

There was still one more person to see. I had been hoping Kelly would be at my dad's 80th birthday celebration. After 15 long years, I had finally planned to speak to her, to bridge the gap between us. But she wasn't there.

When my niece asked if I would like to see her mum, I didn't hesitate, I was unsure of how it would feel after all this time, but I said yes. Soon, I found myself standing in front of her, heart racing, emotions swirling. The moment I saw her, a wave of joy washed over me, and before I knew it, we were in each other's arms, holding on tight. I cried happy tears that had been waiting for this very moment.

There was something in the air that day, something beyond us. A quiet, powerful sense of change and peace, like time had finally softened the edges, making room for healing.

In June I had a dream that Teresa gave us a surprise visit by entering the house through the back door. Luke was keeping the secret. He picked her up from the airport and we were sitting on the couch and Teresa entered the house through the back door while Luke came from the front door. We were so surprised. My heart was jumping for joy. This dream came true. I thanked Jesus for bringing my children back to me. Unfortunately, Teresa was just visiting for two weeks. For those two weeks, I was so happy. I stayed in the moment feeling my heart full with joy. We supported Mick's football team, which Xavier was part of. It was exciting to have my family together.

Jane and I worked together on the India itinerary, planning a trip for the whole family. She took care of all the bookings, flights, accommodations, sightseeing, and even arranged for a driver for a month-long stay, mostly in North India. My in-laws came over to help out and made sure everything at home was looked after while we were away. Teresa joined us from the UK for two and a half weeks, and I was overjoyed when I saw her walk through the doors of the Delhi airport. It felt so good to be reunited twice in the same year and I couldn't wait to spend time with her again.

The driver met us at the airport and navigated through the thick Delhi traffic. As I watched the chaos unfold around us, the cars, bikes, and auto-rickshaws weaving in and out with non-stop honking, I wondered how we were ever going to make it to the hotel. But to my surprise, we arrived in a timely manner, despite the madness on the roads.

When we reached the hotel, a young man came to help with our suitcases. Mick, ever the protective and organised one, immediately said, "No, it's okay," as he gripped one suitcase tightly. I couldn't help but laugh inside as

I watched them, Mick on one side of the suitcase, the young man on the other, both refusing to let go. Mick was so worried the guy might steal it or do something, but in reality, the man was just trying to help. Mick, with all his research and careful planning, was so hyper-aware of everything. Little did he know, he really didn't need to worry here.

The next day, we set out for the Taj Mahal. As soon as it came into view, I was awestruck. The beauty of the Taj was beyond words, and I couldn't believe I was finally standing before one of the Seven Wonders of the World. We took so many photos, even sitting on the bench where Lady Diana once sat. Walking through the grounds, touching the cool marble, and seeing the intricate details up close, I marvelled at what love could create so many centuries ago. Shah Jahan built this tomb for his beloved wife, Mumtaz Mahal. Thousands of people were lined up to go inside, and in that moment, my heart swelled with joy. I was in India with my family, experiencing something extraordinary, and I knew the next four weeks would be filled with more wonders and discoveries.

As I stood there, my thoughts turned to my grandfather Aja and my great-grandfather, my mum's grandfather, who had left India long ago to make a life in Fiji. Every day of this trip, I felt their presence more strongly. I thought of their struggles, their bravery, and the courage it must have taken to leave their parents, their homes, and everything familiar to start anew in a distant land. This journey was not only about seeing India; it was about connecting with my roots and honouring the legacy left behind by my ancestors, people I had never met.

India had everything, not just the cows wandering freely on the streets, the piles of rubbish on the ground, or the stark contrast between the poorest of the poor and the incredibly wealthy. It was a land bursting with life, flavour, and colour. The food was an explosion of spices, which was so familiar, and the people were kind, their beauty shining through in every smile. As I walked through the bustling streets, I felt an immense gratitude for my ancestors, who left India and paved the way for the life I have now.

We arrived home three days before Christmas. My in-laws had everything organised. It felt so good to celebrate my favourite time of year with a house full of people, especially with Luke back this year. The energy in the air was joyful, and I felt blessed to have everyone together under one roof again, except Teresa.

After celebrating New Year's, I took Luke to Brisbane to have a pterygium removed from his eye—a condition that was getting worse and had to be surgically treated. I was scared for him. This disease usually affects older people and seeing him suffer was hard to watch. We stayed at Jane's house while I nursed him through his recovery. He was in so much pain, and I felt utterly helpless. All I could do was pray for his full recovery, hoping he would soon return to doing what he loved most, playing football. Thankfully, after three months, Luke made a full recovery. He stayed in Brisbane, found a job, joined a football team, and made a home there. Though I missed having him close, I was proud to see him thriving in a new city, following his passion. At least he was in the same country.

In February, I received a phone call from my sister. Dad had a heart attack and was in the hospital, recovering after a stent procedure. For a moment, I feared the worst, thinking I might never get to see him again, as I had to fly to Melbourne. But thank God, he pulled through, and I was able to visit him at home. It was such a relief to see him, but something strange happened to me. My back went out, and I could hardly walk. Kerrie had to wheel me in a wheelchair to the departure gate. I think the shock of hearing about Dad had jolted my system, and I ended up bedridden for two weeks when I came back home. I had to completely rest, and during that time, Friday lady had to take over my shifts at work. I did my L5 nerve damage, which the doctor told me would take six weeks to heal. I thought to myself, who has six weeks to heal from back pain? I went back to work after three weeks and somehow managed my tasks.

Lying there, unable to move, I had a moment of realisation. I needed to take care of myself, both my body and my mind. The scare with Dad, and my mums with dementia, made me see that I couldn't keep going without looking after my health. When I finally returned to work, Jenny had done such a great job that it sparked an idea. Maybe it was time for me to think about doing something else with my life, something different, something more aligned with taking care of my soul's desire.

Meanwhile, a job came up working two days a week as a counsellor, and I applied for it thinking I have nothing to lose and I got it. I believe Jesus sent me to St Joseph's school, and I was so grateful that the principal gave me the opportunity. On the other three days, I was in the Tuck shop. On Saturdays, I volunteered at Jamie Oliver's food van for weeks, where I learned so much about cooking and how I could use those skills to teach kids at school to prepare healthy meals. From there, I started the Stephanie Alexander Cooking and Gardening Program, which was an incredible experience.

Not long after, when the principal was overseas, I was informed by the Catholic Diocese that I needed to obtain a certificate in counselling if I wanted to continue in that role. They urged me to enrol in the course immediately, but I refused and ultimately had to step down. It was then in my disappointment that I decided to pursue a long-held dream, I enrolled at CQ university to study for an education degree. Before I could begin, I had to complete four preparatory subjects for nine months to meet the requirements for teaching in Australia as I didn't go to school here.

I was incredibly excited. This was my chance to fulfill my dream of becoming a teacher. Although the coursework was tough, I loved every minute of learning. I formed a study group, and we often went out for lunch after hours of studying. It felt like my mind was being stretched in ways I hadn't experienced before. I'd come home after classes and spend hours studying, driven by a newfound passion for learning. I enjoyed math thanks to the amazing teacher from Melbourne who loved teaching and we both later found out that he missed out on having his wedding on the same day as me at St Joseph's church in Chelsea. We had a good laugh. He had to go to the next church.

And then, even more wonderful news arrived, Helen's daughter, our goddaughter, was getting married in Bali, Indonesia. My in-laws came from Darwin as they were travelling around Australia to take care of Xavier as he wanted to stay with granny and grandad. I was so blessed to have my in-laws in my life. I asked Teresa if she would like to join us for the wedding, and she excitedly agreed. The experience was magical, Bali, with its stunning landscapes and warm atmosphere, provided the perfect backdrop for such a joyful occasion.

We fell in love with the island, the warmth of the people, the vibrant flavours of the food, and the beauty that seemed to be everywhere we turned. But more than anything, it was the company that made the experience so special. Spending time with Mick, Teresa, her partner, Luke, Kerrie, and friends in such a magical setting filled my heart with happiness. Surrounded by my loved ones, celebrating such a joyous event, I couldn't help but feel my heart overflow with gratitude.

We came home to a house full of people—my in-laws, my three children, and an extra one, Teresa's partner. For a moment, as I looked around, my heart swelled with contentment. This was what I truly desired: my family, the people I loved most, all gathered together. I wanted them close, under one roof, sharing life's everyday moments. My heart was full, knowing this was the life my soul had dreamed of for the last couple of years.

After everyone left, I immersed myself in my studies, finding joy in the work and often losing track of time as I dove deeper into the subjects. It became a welcome distraction from the emptiness I sometimes felt. In December, Xavier finished primary school, and I got really emotional thinking about him moving on, no longer being at the same school as me. I worried about how he would stay safe in high school. Still, I was incredibly proud of him, especially on the last day when he and a Grade Six girl stood in front of a packed church, speaking to parents and families about their journey from Prep to Grade Six. Watching him, I was filled with love and pride—God had truly gifted him with a remarkable voice and a creative mind. On Sundays, he would busk at the market, and I found so much joy in sitting there, listening to him play guitar and sing.

For my 50th celebration we went to Magnetic Island, and it felt like magic. Luke and Jane, along with her new partner, came up from Brisbane, and Kerrie flew in from Melbourne. Five of my dear friends from Townsville joined us as well. The night was spent at the Stage Door Show, and it was the best night of my life. Jane had everyone up and dancing, bringing this incredible energy to the evening. We laughed, danced, and even chatted with strangers who felt like friends by the end of the night. It was as if the entire room was celebrating with me, like one big family.

The highlight of the night was when Luke and I were called up on stage. I felt like a princess, with all eyes on me, surrounded by so much love. My heart was full, overflowing with joy, and for once, I let myself truly relax in the warmth of it all.

In the days that followed, Kerrie and I cherished the quiet moments together. We went to yoga classes, enjoyed long breakfasts, and had some peaceful swims with Mick and Xavier while the rest of the group went back home. It was the perfect way to unwind after such a wonderful celebration, a balance of fun and serenity that I needed to begin the next chapter of my life.

I passed all my subjects, but when it came to the IELTS test, I fell short by one mark. The disappointment hit me hard, and I couldn't shake the feeling that I had failed. Eventually, it became too much. It felt like the weight of everything on my plate was crashing down on me, working in the tuck shop, running the Stephanie Alexander program, managing a business, and holding the household together. I had to let go of my studies, and mentally, I spiralled, blaming that monster once again in Fiji.

Weeks passed before I could gather the strength to put my faith in Jesus, to trust that everything would work out in its own time. I continued working two days a week, running the gardening and cooking program. Despite everything, I found peace in that space, working in the garden with the children, planting seeds, watering, harvesting, and then cooking together. We would all sit around a big table, sharing the food we had cooked. The children absolutely loved the hands-on experience, and so did I. It was a small sanctuary in the middle of all the chaos.

Not long after, Teresa flew to Melbourne, and I followed to meet her and spend time with the family. One of the highlights was taking my second mum to see the musical Aladdin with Teresa. It was a magical experience. Watching the show together and having my daughter back with me made it even more special. The three of us cherished every moment spent together.

Soon after, Teresa and I flew to Brisbane to plan Luke's 21st birthday at the Story Bridge Hotel. My heart was full as I had my whole family together to celebrate such an important milestone. Luke's granny and his cousins, Kerrie and her family, came from Melbourne, as Kerrie had celebrated her 50th on the Gold Coast a week earlier. My favourite auntie and her family drove from Sydney to join in the festivities. Everyone had an amazing night, one that we will always remember, and I couldn't have been happier seeing Luke surrounded by so much love and joy.

Three months later, we received news: Kerrie had breast cancer, and it was serious. I was devastated. How could Kerrie, of all people, have cancer? She was a vegan, exercised regularly, and was deeply spiritual. It didn't make sense. This couldn't be happening to my best friend. I felt a flood of disbelief and sorrow, and all I could do was pray for Kerrie's health, asking Jesus to give her strength and healing.

Meanwhile, my eldest sister, auntie, and uncle came over from Melbourne for a visit. Their presence was a balm to my heavy heart. It was so good to have them here. We cooked together, took a trip to Magnetic Island, spent time laughing, and truly enjoyed each other's company. Despite the weight of the news, those moments with family brought much-needed comfort.

In December, when school finished, Xavier and I flew to Melbourne so I could spend some time with Kerrie, but a week later, devastating news shattered that plan. My second mum had been diagnosed with pancreatic cancer. The news was grave, and the weight of it pulled us all down. Luke joined us, and Mick soon followed, but it was the worst Christmas we had ever experienced. My second mum was in the hospital, gravely ill, and there was nothing we could do to take away her pain.

Kerrie was already battling breast cancer, and now her mother faced this cruel disease too. My heart was breaking into pieces as I watched the two most important people in my life suffer. I wanted to take away their pain, but I was helpless.

My mum was in agony after falling out of bed and injuring her back. She could barely walk, and seeing her struggle only deepened my heartache. My mind and soul were overwhelmed with the pain of it all—watching the women I loved so much endure unbearable suffering, knowing there was nothing I could do to ease it. I had to put my deep pain aside, hoping it would disappear if I just buried it deep inside, amongst all the other pain I was carrying. I went to my sister's house to see my mum, as my sister was caring for her. Predator showed up, and my stomach dropped, but I had to sit there and pretend I was okay. I told myself again, "It's not about you, Gyan. Don't be selfish. Mum is in so much pain; your pain will go away in time. No one can see your pain. It's okay."

My second mum had the operation in January, and the very next day after visiting her in the hospital, I had to go home. My heart ached as I stood by her bedside, watching her frail body tangled in tubes, helpless in her pain. It was all I could do—just stand there, my chest heavy with sorrow. To make things worse, Kerrie was in the same hospital undergoing chemotherapy for breast cancer. Leaving them both behind was unbearable, but I had no choice.

In May, I returned to spend more time with my second mum while she was back in the hospital. By then, it was clear she wanted to go home to die. Somehow, she trusted me to take care of her, and I found strength I didn't know I had. The operation hadn't worked, and four months later, she passed away. I still don't know where I found the strength to wash and change her with my father-in-law's help. It was the hardest thing I've ever done, but Jesus carried me through each moment. I did it for Kerrie and for myself.

Teresa flew in from the UK to help, taking over nursing her granny, which allowed me to go back home. My beautiful second mum passed away the very next day. Mick never got to say goodbye in person—his flight was in the evening, but she left us in the afternoon. The grief weighed so heavily on me, and I still miss her so much.

My heart ached. I texted my sister, telling her that if I ever had to take care of our own mum, I would. I had let go of my anger toward her for not supporting me through my pain, and I had forgiven her.

Chapter 12

My Healing

I used to stay broken hearted like it was my job and destiny, staying sad was all I knew, and it kept me safe. Self-denial was how I earned my worthiness and suffering was my comfort zone. I lived in my head a lot with anxiety in my stomach. Feeling and blaming myself when things went wrong in my life, always asking poor quality questions like - why did this happen to me? How come nobody supported me? I did nothing wrong. Where was the Lord?

There are billions of people on this planet, and just two of them hurt me. So why would I let those two people overshadow the beautiful experiences life has to offer? It sounds crazy now, but for many years, I didn't know what to do with these feelings. I didn't know how to get rid of this pain until I began working on myself. I thought if I bury it deep within, I will be fine and the pain will go away. I moved from one country to another, one state to another, but this pain never went away.

In February 2019, after the floods came to Townsville, I found myself drowning—not just in water, but in my emotions. I was terrified, feeling as though I was losing control. It was in that fragile state that I made a commitment to love myself and do whatever it took to heal from the inside out. I would lie in my bed and would sew my heart back using cotton and thread every night before falling asleep. This process helped a lot. My broken heart started to heal. That's when I stumbled upon Kelly Hine on Facebook, offering five to ten minute meditations. Desperate for peace, I dove in completely, and those short meditations calmed my anxious heart.

I joined Kelly Hine's group called Soul Space, where she combined guided meditation with journaling. Slowly, I felt something shift. A glimmer of peace sparked within me, and for the first time in a long while, I believed I could heal. The shame and guilt I'd carried like a sack of rocks on my back felt lighter. I found peace and connection in this group of soul sisters; women who offered the support I had longed for. It felt like I'd found my tribe.

I started working on this session, *How to Forgive When You Don't Feel Like It*. It outlined four important steps to forgiveness: Repentance, Forgiveness, Gratitude, and Love—each with its own profound power. I decided to make this my mantra:

- I'm sorry
- Please forgive me
- Thank you
- I love you

Every morning, as soon as I got out of bed, I would go to the mirror and recite these words. At first, it felt awkward, even forced. But gradually, I began to smile and truly believe in the power of those words. They became part of me, a daily practice that opened my heart a little more each time.

Kelly's meditations were transformative. Her gentle guidance during each session made it easy to quiet my mind and focus. Afterward, she would encourage us to journal our thoughts. At first, I didn't know what journaling your thoughts meant, allowing whatever surfaced to flow freely onto the page. That simple exercise of writing out my emotions became a game changer.

During those meditations, I began the difficult task of forgiving my mother and each family member who hadn't been there for me at my lowest. It was painful, stirring up memories and emotions I'd long buried, but I stayed with the process. Each time I meditated, I asked Jesus for strength, praying for the courage to release the bitterness I had carried for so long. I thanked Him for guiding me to the right people at the right time—people who were helping me heal from the trauma that had weighed on me for so many years. Gradually, through the meditations and journaling, I felt the heavy burden of resentment and pain lift, replaced by a growing sense of peace and love.

Healing is an ongoing process; it takes time to work through the layers of deep trauma. I don't know if you ever completely heal, but one thing I have learned is that you cannot do it on your own. You need support—people who will walk beside you, encourage you, and remind you of your strength. It's through their presence and my faith that I am learning to let go and move forward, one small step at a time.

In August, I travelled to Melbourne to celebrate my mum's 80th birthday. By now, she had become very fragile, her body weighed down by the years. She still knew everyone's name, and for that, I was grateful. Yet, her emotions seemed to overwhelm her—she cried often, but words rarely came. It was heartbreaking to see her this way, a shadow of the strong woman I once knew. All I wanted

MY HEALING

to do was hold her, tell her how much I loved her, and let her know everything was okay now. I had let it all go. I was doing fine. But I wasn't sure if she could understand, and that uncertainty ached inside me. That's the last time I saw my mum.

By September 2019, we were in a different place—not just emotionally, but physically. We took a six week holiday to Singapore, with Luke joining us. Then, the four of us flew to the UK to visit Teresa and her partner. Being reunited with my family filled me with such happiness; I felt like the luckiest mother on the planet. After the UK, we travelled to Austria and Croatia with Teresa and her partner for a week. The time we spent together, exploring new places, felt like a beautiful gift. After they left, the four of us continued our journey, discovering more of Croatia and Slovenia on our own, before returning to the UK to spend more time with Teresa.

2020, COVID came and turned everyone's life upside down. I was deeply worried about Teresa and wanted her to come home as the virus spread and people were dying all over the world. In the midst of this fear, I received a message from my sister—my mum was in the hospital, very sick. My heart told me to drop everything and go to her, but with COVID restrictions, I hesitated.

My sister faced timed me from the hospital so I could speak to Mum. When I asked her if she knew who I was, she responded without hesitation, "Gyan". Hearing her say my name filled me with relief and joy—I was so happy she remembered me. That moment would be the last time I spoke to her.

All I could think about was going to her, holding her hand, and telling her how much I loved her, that it was okay, that we all make mistakes. But time slipped away, and I missed my chance. With no direct flights to Melbourne, Xavier and I flew to Brisbane, where we stayed with Luke and Mary for a couple of days before we could get a flight. By then, my mum had been moved to aged care, and we had to get flu injections just to be allowed to visit her.

The next morning, I woke up and saw 19 missed calls on my phone. I knew something was terribly wrong. My mum hadn't waited for me. She left us at 11:30 p.m. on the 28th of April in 2020.

My heart shattered. I felt as though I was plunged into a dark place, consumed by grief. I howled and screamed uncontrollably, as if the sky had fallen and trapped me beneath it. I was lost in my emotions. Never in my life have I felt that much grief. My chest was hurting, unsure of how to move forward.

I gathered all my strength. Xavier and I walked to the shop to pick up some pastry so I could keep my promise to Mary and give her a cooking lesson. We spent the afternoon cooking together—samosas, butter chicken, and vegetables—filling the kitchen with warmth and familiar scents. As I stood there, teaching Mary, I felt my mum with me, giving me the strength to keep going, as though her presence were guiding my hands.

We stayed at Kerrie's house for three weeks and during that time, she took care of us, helping me stay grounded through the whirlwind of emotions. But the next day, I had to face what I'd been dreading. When I visited my mum at the funeral home, seeing her lying in the coffin was heart-wrenching. I took her hand, and I don't know what I was expecting—maybe a trace of warmth, something—but her hand was cold, and it hit me hard. She was truly gone.

Through my tears, I told her how much I loved her. Then, with shaky hands, I applied makeup to her face, carefully putting on her lipstick. It felt like a privilege to do this for her, to share this intimate moment before saying my last goodbye. Only close family could be there, ten people at a time, but it was enough. We were together—my dad, his four daughters, a son, a niece, an aunt, an uncle, and the priest—celebrating her life in the way she deserved.

The day of the funeral was difficult, but it was also peaceful in an unexpected way. For the first time in so long, I could relax and grieve without the presence of the predator. I thanked God for the space He gave me to mourn my mum in peace, something I had been yearning for but always missed out on during family gatherings. Now, in spirit, she was with us all.

As the coffin was placed in the car, a wild, uncontrollable urge surged through me—I wanted to run after it, to stay with her, to not let go. My feelings were overwhelming, a heavy tide of grief pulling me under, but somehow, I knew that even though she was gone, she was still with me in a different way. It was as if her spirit was gently helping me find the strength to carry on.

For the next 13 days, we sat together as a family, listening to the priest recite and translate the verses of the Bhagavad Gita every night. The words were soothing to my soul, offering a kind of peace that seemed to reach into the very depths of my grief. It was as though the ancient wisdom was wrapping itself around my sorrow, softening the edges, and giving me the comfort I desperately needed. I was so grateful that, even during the Covid pandemic, I could be there with my family, sharing this sacred time together. The distance and isolation that so many others endured felt lessened by the strength we found in each other's presence and the connection to something greater than ourselves.

When I came back home, there were days when all I wanted to do was sit in a corner, curled up in a fetal position, and shut out the world. The mental weight

MY HEALING

was crushing. I kept thinking I should have told her earlier how much I loved her. I should have broken my promise to myself. The pain in my chest was sometimes unbearable, and the sadness in my heart was so heavy that continuing felt impossible. Luckily, my family and work kept me going. My friends, the children at school, and my responsibilities got me out of bed each day.

Jane and I started doing morning exercise classes three times a week through Zoom, using body tappers to stimulate energy led by Kerrie. We also did deep spiritual work, cleansing our chakras and practicing meditation, which helped ground me. These small acts of connection and self-care made it easier to get up every morning. I continued engaging with my soul space sisters with Kelly Hine every week with live sessions through meditations and journaling, finding a bit of peace in that shared space. For physical health I did Pilates and yoga classes at the gym.

Swimming also became part of my healing journey. I set myself a goal to swim the length of the pool, attending weekly lessons and practicing with a friend. It stemmed from a moment in Croatia when my whole family swam from a boat to a small island. The boat couldn't get close to the beach, so they swam, but I stayed behind, frozen with fear of the water. That fear motivated me to take lessons so I wouldn't find myself stuck in that helpless place again.

With COVID restrictions in place, we began exploring closer to home, and I set myself a new challenge: snorkelling in the open ocean. We travelled to Airlie Beach and took a small raft to Whitehaven Beach, where we snorkelled in the magical underwater world. I wore a life jacket, and Mick stayed close to reassure me I'd be fine. That moment planted a seed of courage. Sometime later, I snorkelled at Fitzroy Island off Cairns, wearing a life jacket without feeling silly—because the joy I felt in the ocean, experiencing the beauty of nature, far outweighed any fear.

The first time my friend invited me to go kayaking in the river, I hesitated. I expected to wear a life jacket, but she believed in me more than I did myself. "You'll be fine," she said. I've since kayaked confidently without a life jacket, and those moments have helped me grow stronger.

Sometimes, you just need a helping hand to keep moving forward. I am so grateful for my beautiful friends who have always been there for me, lifting me up when I needed it most.

While I was in the midst of healing, unfortunately my integrity was questioned. When the school principal was suspended without any explanation, we were all shocked. It was a week filled with uncertainty and fear as we imagined the worst. I was working as a teacher aide in Grade Five. Two students, close friends, wrote a note accusing me of inappropriately touching them and gave it to the teacher. I was called into the office by the acting principal during lunch, and when I heard the news, it hit me like a ton of bricks.

I had walked into the office thinking I was there to discuss helping pay for a student's camp fee because the mother couldn't afford it. I had no idea what was waiting for me. It felt like a bad dream, but there was no waking up from this. As the principal spoke, an accusation I never saw coming was laid before me, heavy and piercing. I felt the air go cold around me, words slipping away as I tried to understand what was happening.

Stunned, I stumbled back to the staff room, barely making it to a chair before the tears I'd been holding back broke free. I felt devastated, completely lost, and a churning ache opened inside me. Deep down, I knew the accusation was wrong, yet my mind kept racing. How was I supposed to prove my innocence? The very idea of being wrongfully accused rekindled old pain I hadn't let surface in years—the unresolved fight of my 16-year-old self, the one who had tried so desperately to find justice but never did.

The memories, raw and relentless, brought a strange new resolve within me. We were encouraged to see a counsellor because of everything happening at the school with the principal, and for the first time, I went. It took every ounce of strength to sit down with the counsellor at a women's centre and tell her about my life at 16. I didn't even know how the words would come out, yet they did, piece by piece. When I finished, she looked at me with a softness in her eyes and said, "You did everything you could to keep yourself safe by locking that back door. You were in your own home. You weren't to blame."

In that moment, something deep inside shifted. I wasn't out at night; I wasn't somewhere I shouldn't have been. I was just a young girl, safe at home, doing everything right, and still, somehow, it had all gone wrong. I realised then that I'd spent too many years silently suffering, weighed down by shame and guilt that never belonged to me in the first place.

The counsellor's words stirred up a sense of courage I didn't know I had left. That's when I realised, I should have asked for help long ago instead of suffering silently. I got empowered for the first time to use my voice to speak my truth and found strength to tell some of the staff.

For the next six months, I struggled to stay afloat. What kept me going, though, were the children's achievements, each one like a small light breaking through the clouds. Their growth, their triumphs, brought me more joy than I could express. I thought about reaching my ten-year mark at the school I cherished so deeply, and the dream I held close—to stay there until well past retirement, surrounded by the place and the people I loved.

MY HEALING

What also kept me going was my time in the park, a quiet sanctuary filled with towering trees and a serene pond dotted with lily pads and alive with birds and ducks. Often, I'd slip off my shoes and let the earth ground me, feeling the cool grass beneath my feet as I lay back, connecting with Mother Gaia's energy. Some days, I would sit beneath a tree, feeling its bark against my back, or wrap my arms around its sturdy trunk, letting the stillness and strength of nature anchor me. On sunny days, I'd lie on the grass, eyes open, sun gazing, seeing beautiful chakra colours, soaking up the warmth and peace it brought from within. These small, sacred rituals renewed me, providing strength when I needed it most.

Jenny and I often talked together in the tuckshop, musing that the kids we cared for today would someday take care of us in our old age with the same love, kindness, and compassion we gave them. We liked to imagine them all grown up, still holding a soft spot for the familiar faces who'd been there during their most formative years.

But the hardest part of all this turmoil was knowing just how much I adored my job and the connections I'd built. It felt unthinkable to leave. In the end, though, the decision couldn't be avoided. I had to make the heartbreaking choice to walk away, leaving behind the place, the friends, and the memories that had meant the world to me for a decade.

That's when I found a new path. With no other options on the horizon, I channelled my passion into starting my own business—catering. And from there, a new chapter began.

I dug deep into my healing journey and discovered a well of anger within me—anger at the injustices inflicted by others. The unfairness, the needless suffering—it had all been buried deep, but it was still there, a raw and burning wound. I came to understand that this anger, perhaps, could be harnessed and shaped into something less destructive and more purposeful. It didn't have to consume me.

Anger, I realised, is like any skill—it can be honed and expressed in ways that bring release, not harm. I wondered if I could channel it into something beautiful, like singing. Maybe, by joining a choir, I could vocalise the unspoken hurt in a more refined and enchanting way. So, I took that step and joined the church choir. It wasn't just about singing hymns; it was a way to release the storm within me, to let my soul find peace amidst the music.

In that sacred space, I found peace. Yet my favourite healing place became my visits to what I affectionately call "Jesus' clinic." It's where I often pray and ask Jesus to place his healing hands on me, to lift the burden of my pain so I can, in turn, help others. Each visit brought a new layer of healing, a quiet but profound transformation.

MY HEALING

Healing is an ongoing journey, one that requires patience, courage, resilience, and an unwavering commitment to oneself. I am still healing, still working through those memories that occasionally pull me back to some of the darker moments in my life. But now, there's a difference—I know I am in control. I am the master of my own destiny.

Today, I feel stronger than I've ever been, with a newfound pride in everything I've achieved. I've realised that the most crucial part of this journey is not how others see me, but how I see myself, how I remain true to who I am. What matters most is the love I've discovered within myself, a love no longer dependent on external sources but deeply rooted in my faith and the grace of God.

Every step forward is a reminder of this love, of this power, and of the strength that comes from honouring my truth.

Afterword

When I first began writing this memoir, I was hesitant to revisit the past, to open old wounds, and to face the memories that I had long tucked away. But as the words began to flow, so did the tears of healing. Writing became a way to reclaim my story, to honour the struggles, and to celebrate the victories, no matter how small.

I'm reminded that life rarely goes as planned. The detours, heartaches, and unexpected joys are what make our stories uniquely ours. If there is one thing I've learned, it's that resilience is born not from avoiding pain but from embracing it—learning to dance in the rain even when the storm rages on. I've realised that healing is not a destination but a journey. The wounds of the past may never fully disappear, but I am grateful for the strength they've given me. Sharing my story has been both a release and a revelation, reminding me that the power of vulnerability can forge deeper connections than I ever imagined.

To those who feel lost or broken, I want you to know that you are not broken. You need help, my friends—don't suffer in silence. Find a safe place first; you can't stay in a toxic and unloved environment, as your soul will always be searching for love and connection. And remember, there is always hope and resilience lies within us all even in the darkest hours. The road to healing may be long and winding, but it is worth every step. You are not alone in your struggles, and sharing my story is my way of standing with you wherever you are on your journey.

Thank you for allowing me to share my life with you. It is my hope that these pages have offered a glimpse of light, a sense of solidarity, and perhaps even the courage to write your own story.

The journey continues. This is not the end but a new beginning. I look forward to what the future holds, embracing every twist and turn with Jesus in my heart.

About the Author

Born amidst the stunning landscapes of the Fiji Islands, Gyan has embraced Australia as her home for over four decades. Her life is a vibrant tapestry of family, food, and exploration. A devoted wife of 34 years and a proud mother, Gyan's warmth and creativity shine through in all she does—most notably in the culinary delights she shares from her lively food truck, GG's Bhojan.

A passionate adventurer at heart, Gyan and her husband have travelled to 33 countries, immersing themselves in diverse cultures that inspire her cooking and storytelling. Gyan and her husband are also embarking on an exciting new venture, ECO Trilogy, to champion environmental care and sustainability.

Beyond her entrepreneurial endeavours, Gyan is deeply rooted in her community. She volunteers with the St. Vincent de Paul Society and actively participates in her local church, finding joy in giving back. Her life is a testament to the power of love, resilience, and the simple joy of sharing good food and meaningful stories with the world. Through her writing, she seeks to uplift and inspire, weaving hope and a touch of magic into every chapter of her journey.

ABOUT THE AUTHOR

Note

Gyan's children are forging exciting paths of their own. Teresa had been living in the UK for over a decade with her partner and is now settled back in Australia, mastering life's practicalities and building a bright future. Luke, based in Brisbane, is growing a company called Green Care with his cousin, all while pursuing his lifelong passion for football. He and his wife Mary, are expecting their first child, adding a new blessing to the family. Xavier has recently moved out to share a home with his partner and friends. A talented musician, he teaches at several Catholic schools, studies for an education degree, and finds time to perform in musicals any chance he gets. Gyan eagerly anticipates the day she becomes Aji and Nani.

Acknowledgments

I am deeply grateful to Jesus for His guidance, wisdom, and love, which have transformed my life and given me the strength to write this book. My prayer is that these pages inspire you, give you courage, and invite you to welcome the Lord into your life, letting Him walk with you every day.

To my parents, for doing their best for me and helping me to realise that it's up to me to do my best and find love from within.

To my dearest friend Helen, thank you for being so kind and loving when I needed a friend the most, and for introducing me to Jesus. Your compassion and faith have had a lasting impact on my life.

To my beloved husband, who was truly sent by Jesus to find me and love me unconditionally—I am forever thankful for you. Your commitment and support have been my rock, and I cherish every moment we share. Special thanks to Kerrie, who persisted in introducing her brother to me, even when I said no three times.

To my three beautiful children, who chose me to be their mother—you fill my life with endless joy and purpose. As we embark on this new chapter of becoming grandparents, I am beyond blessed to see our family grow.

To my two soul sisters, Kerrie and Jane, your love, support and encouragement have been a beacon of light in my life. You both inspire me in my journey of healing, and I am so grateful for your friendship.

To Neelam and Jaden, thank you for coming into my life and bringing so much joy. Neelam, your meticulous work in checking my manuscripts and holding my hand throughout this journey has been invaluable.

To my wonderful neighbours, Jan and John, thank you for inviting me to join the book club all those years ago. Jan, your constant support and encouragement every step of the way has meant the world to me. My book club friends, thanks for all your love, support, laughter, and conversations.

ACKNOWLEDGMENTS

To all my friends who have always listened with patience and kindness when I needed to share my story, especially Deb, your understanding has been a true blessing.

Grace Tame for paving the path and giving me courage to tell my story to inspire others so I too can give voice to the voiceless, especially to my niece and all the young girls out there.

To my church community, thank you for embracing me with open arms, for your prayers, and for the spiritual nourishment you provide. Your love and fellowship have been a great source of strength.

To Natasa Denman, and the entire mentoring and publishing team at Ultimate 48 Hour Author — I am deeply grateful. Thank you for believing in me, for your unwavering support, and for guiding me every step of the way. I couldn't have made it here without you.

I am forever grateful to each and every one of you for the roles you've played in my life. This book would not have been possible without your love, support, and faith. Thank you from the bottom of my heart.

To all my families, my heart is still full of love for each and everyone.

To those who have walked beside me, whether in the past or present, thank you for your unwavering support. Your love has been my anchor through the storms. And to you, the reader, thank you for joining me on this deeply personal journey. I hope that by sharing my story, you found a part of your own reflected within these pages.

Speaker Bio

Gyan Russell is the author of *Never an Indian Bride*, a powerful and inspiring book that encourages young girls and women to embrace their authentic selves and live a life true to their values. Passionate about empowering others, Gyan is on a mission to motivate women to cultivate self-love and begin their journey of healing from past traumas.

Aspiring to be a keynote speaker, Gyan aims to share her insights and experiences at events, inspiring audiences to unlock their potential and to lead fulfilling lives. Her heartfelt message resonates with women seeking to rediscover their strength, prioritize their well-being, and overcome challenges with resilience and grace.

Additional Information and Resources

For domestic and family violence support in Australia:
DVConnect Womensline: 1800811811
DVConnect Mensline: 1800600636

Support for victims of abuse (including sexual assault, child abuse) in Queensland:
https://www.qld.gov.au/community/getting-support-health-social-issue/support-victims-abuse

For recovery from childhood abuse:
Bravehearts (Queensland) offer support for adult survivors of child sexual abuse via their Information and Support Line 1800272831

https:bravehearts.org.au/get-help/support-adult-survivors/support-us/

For support with grief:
https://www.grief.org.au/ga/ga/support/Support-Groups.aspx

Grief Australia at 0392652100/ Free call number at 1800642066. https://griefline.org.au/

For mental health support:
For mental health and psychological support: www.beyondblue.org.au
For depression: https://www.blackdoginstitute.org.au/

"Find inner happiness and live on purpose: Soul Space": website: https://kellyhine.com/

Energy and Sound Emporium - Healing and meditation/meditation and breathwork
Facebook link - https://www.facebook.com/energyandsoundemporium

Notes

NEVER AN INDIAN BRIDE

NOTES

www.ingramcontent.com/pod-product-compliance
Lightning Source LLC
Chambersburg PA
CBHW061217070526
44584CB00029B/3871